To my 96 year-old mother

'à table'

These two words still resound in my memory as a prelude to delight.
When my mother shouted the magical words - 'à table les enfants!',
I was the first to rush to the dining table. Always hungry, breathing
in the delicious aromas of the chicken roasting in the oven or the
crème caramel which would make my day, I was the happiest girl
in the world. I still experience the same thrill of pleasure each time
I come to the table, especially if friends are joining me. This is why I
chose this title, which symbolizes two of my favourite ways of being:
sharing and enjoying.

'à table' is an invitation to share the delights of a good meal.
Bon appétit

 **WARNING**
This book is garlic free.
Garlic kills the vampires but it also slays whisky.

Published by AILSAPRESS 2016
Port Charlotte Isle of Islay PA48 7TS
www.ailsapress.com

Illustration credits:
All facing page photographs in the Recipe Section and page 159 by John Paul; other photographs by the author.
The photo on page 146 is by Anna Bush Crews.

Graphic Design by Laurien Stam.
Printed by Grafistar BV Netherlands
www.grafistar.nl

Bon appétit

Martine

à table
whisky from glass to plate

Martine Nouet

with the support of Walkers Shorbread

PRODUCT OF SCOTLAND
Walkers
·· ESTABLISHED 1898 ··

CONTENTS

THANKS TO...

This book would certainly not exist without the encouragements of members of the whisky and food industry who showed their interest and support in food and whisky pairing as well as cooking. I could not name them all but I will give a special mention to Jim Walker and his company Walkers Shortbread who have sponsored the photography. I would like to thank Ann Miller, International Brand Ambassador with Chivas Brothers who has showed a particular enthusiasm for my whisky dinners and helped me to design dinners with Aberlour during more than ten years.

Writing, editing and publishing the book 'All by myself' has been a thrilling but also stressing adventure with moments of doubt and discouragement. But I have been wonderfully assisted by generous and competent friends and professionals.
A warm thank to my friends Ishbel Capper and Brigitte Tilleray who have so kindly proofread my manuscript. A special mention to the tremendous work of John Paul the photographer and Eric Obry the chef, assisted by his chef-pâtissier who have been tireless in their labour. Thank you to Ian Law and Brian Wilson from Glenfiddich distillery who have helped John Paul. Thank you to Fiona Boyle and Ros Lewis who have lent cutlery for the photography.

I will not forget to thank my fellow writer friends Becky and Hans Offringa from Netherlands who connected me with a brilliant technical team: Laurien Stam, graphic designer and Joris Brockotter, printer from Grafistar. I am also grateful to my friend Cathy Wilson on Islay who has offered to welcome my book under Ailsa Press, her publishing company.

Last but not least, thank you to 'Alistair', my Macbook laptop for having stayed awake in the long hours of the day and of the night and for having put up with my prose and my heavy files without grumbling too much.

FOREWORD

First, an admission: I am not a big fan of pairing whisky with food. More accurately, I was not a fan until I experienced Martine's inspired choices of both! She is, without any doubt, the world expert in this arcane area of gastronomy and now she is sharing a quarter of a century's diligent research into the subject with the publication of this handsome book.

It is surprisingly difficult to get pairing and cooking with whisky right. There are no absolute guide-lines – although she does advise us to avoid garlic (perhaps unusual in a French woman!). A master chef of my acquaintance advised against using any wine- or vinegar-based sauces in the cooking when pairing it with whisky. I am glad Martine disputes this, since I am fond of wine- and vinegar-based sauces. Likewise oysters: there is an ancient superstition about combining whisky with oysters – goodness knows why, they work perfectly together, especially lightly smoky and maritime malts.

As she writes: 'Pairing whisky and food is all about finding harmony and balance. Choosing the appropriate whiskies to match dishes requires exactly the same efforts as with wine. You need to have some knowledge about the drink. The rest is practice and a question of taste and sensitivity as the technique is entirely based on sensory evaluation.'

Ah, 'sensory evaluation' – the awareness that 'flavour' is not only synonymous with 'taste', it embraces 'smell' and 'touch' (i.e. texture, mouth-feel effect) as well – and when we describe flavour we commonly reach for similes and metaphors relating to food. Considered individually, a whisky and a dish each has its own character; when these characteristics are matched by a master, either to complement one another or to contrast, the effect can be, literally, sensational. As Martine observes: 'When (well) matched, they create additional character, bringing in new flavours. One plus one equals three, not two…'

As well as pairing, À Table is also about cooking with whisky. Born of many years of experimentation the book provides sensible advice and guidance, sixty-odd mouth-watering recipes and suggestions for which whiskies work best with which dishes.

Both a practical guide and an appetising armchair read, authoritative yet friendly, À Table is a delight, and I commend it to you whole-heartedly.

Charles MacLean
Edinburgh, March 2016

THE ART OF PAIRING

From glass to plate

What happens when you feel between two minds? The wise option is probably to make a choice. But what if you can't? This is exactly what I did some twenty years ago. I was a food journalist, meeting chefs, commenting about cooking and thoroughly enjoying that gourmet life.

On a trip to Scotland and a visit to Tamdhu distillery in Speyside, I happened to put my nose in a glass of whisky. This was in 1990. At the time, I did not drink whisky nor had any inclination to do so. But this trip triggered a new passion and even a new way of life.
I started investigating about spirits, mainly whisky but others as well. I read, I learnt, I met the distillers, I tasted frenetically. Within a few months, I realized that my journalist career would take a new turn. I would write about spirits. Soon after, a journalist in France called me 'la Reine de l'alambic' - the Queen of the Still - in a portrait. But what about food? My interest in cooking had not decreased in favour of my involvement with spirits. I wanted to carry on exploring both.

As to keep writing on both subjects, I started experimenting at home. I improvised whisky dinners, inviting friends as guinea-pigs. I also added whisky to dishes, using different techniques and a diverse range of single malts.

I took notes, wrote down recipes. Not all my experiments were successful at first try. But I never gave up. I initiated cooking with malt whisky classes in Paris. These classes were my 'live laboratory'. I designed whisky dinners with chefs, in France first then much further. Today, I tour the world to host dinners as launching events for whisky festivals. But I must say that, at the beginning, I was pacing a desert in an indifferent, if not hostile, environment. At this time, the thought of serving a whisky at the table was considered by marketing departments as a crazy idea: inappropriate, eccentric, so French... It took me years to convince the whisky industry of the mutual enhancement food and whisky could benefit from. I am delighted to note that the 'French touch' is no longer seen as uncalled-for and that a lot of whisky brands include food pairing in their agenda of events.

I go a step forward pairing as I include 'cooking with whisky' in my pairing investigations. Whisky is then considered as a 'seasoning' ingredient, along the same line as herbs or spices.
The book will take you through the seasons with a mouth-watering selection of easy to prepare recipes. For each one, a detailed description of the best whisky to pair with (and to cook with) will be given alongside a suggestion of five whiskies. If pride of place is given to Scottish single malts, Irish whiskeys, single grain whiskies and bourbons, Japanese whiskies or other worldwide whiskies also feature in the suggestions. The 'whisky cook' will thus have the choice between more than 200 whiskies for his/her pairing experiments.

I recommend accompanying desserts with the delicious Walkers Shortbread and cheese with oatcakes. They both match so well with whisky. A 'terroir' pairing with Speyside single malts.
All the recipes have been tested by gourmet palates. I can assure they don't require any particular professional skill. I have never laid claim to be called a chef.
All the dishes have been prepared with panache by Eric Obry, the amazing chef of Le Petit gourmand, a French 'salon de thé' in Aberlour (Speyside) with the collaboration of his chef pâtissier. John Paul, talented photographer, is the other artist who has brought a valuable contribution to the book.

Now it is time for you to enjoy your own experiments and to come to the table. A table!

A world of sensations

Why is 'à table' following the seasons' cycle? Because seasons are the essence of life, they dictate what we are, what we do, what we eat and what we drink.
Yes there is a seasonal character in whiskies as much as tomatoes signify Summer and mushrooms imply Autumn. The exploration of whisky aromas has brought me to give priority to sensory evaluation. When it comes to aromas and flavors, our emotions are extraordinarily linked to our senses. The enjoyment one gets from tasting a good whisky - in moderation, an absolute prerequisite for me - is subject to the sensation each one of us gets from it.

Spring

One word: wake up. Nature is reviving, vegetation shows bright acid colours and flowers soft pastel ones. The air is light and fragrant. We feel full of energy, Vital energies rise. We want freshness, simple and straightforward flavours, enhanced by this revitalizing tangy kick of just ripe fruit and vegetables. Raw, light and crunchy ingredients convey the sensory identity of Spring. Exactly what a 'springtime whisky' will reflect.
We breathe in the season. Spring symbolizes the youth, early morning and an uplifting mood.
Element: air | Sense: smell | Taste: sour

Summer

This is the season of the extreme. Bright colours are exacerbated, fruit and vegetable are colourful, ripe and juicy. The sunny days concentrate textures and flavours, the air is salty. Intensity and depth is the characteristic of summery whiskies. Full-bodied, they show a warm and cheerful character. Bright red, yellow and orange colour the dishes.
We taste and enjoy Summer. It symbolizes the adult age when dreams and ambitions are fulfilled, and one is active and in full command. The time division is midday and the mood is conversational, communicative.
Element: fire | Sense: taste | Taste: salty

Starting from the four seasons, it is fascinating to notice the recurrent pattern of four in anything to do with a life cycle: the four elements, the four seasons, the four times of the day notwithstanding the four stages of a lifespan, which take one from childhood to old age. I have therefore chosen these four stages to take you through the sensory reading of whisky, having added a specific sense and a specific taste to each cycle as well as a specific mood. The mood concept has in fact been developed by Ronnie Cox, director of The Glenrothes to describe the style of Glenrothes whisky vintages.

Autumn

Autumn is the intermediary between being awake and going to sleep. Trees start losing their leaves, days are shorter, the rhythm of life is slower. Nature dresses in amber and golden colours, a delight for the eye. The whisky, older and often matured in sherry casks, is darker too. Autumn is the season of slow-cooked stews, rich sauces, baked fruit and dark chutneys, sometimes slightly overcooked with a bitter edge. Glass and plate colours match. This is the age of maturity when you have no more to prove. You can appreciate a relaxing mood. The time division is the evening.
Element: earth | Sense: sight | Taste: bitter

Winter

There is an air of simplicity and sobriety in winter when snow and ice cover the ground. Not much to see but you can hear, even the silence. This minimalist sensation is also conveyed by the bareness of the vegetation. Nature goes to sleep and looks mineral and austere in white, grey and black colours. By contrast, this austerity invites to enjoy sweet and rich flavours. Old whiskies, with a bitter-sweet oaky note and a lingering finish with intense chocolate call the tune. This is the last quart of a life, old age. The time division is the night, favourable for meditating.
Element: water | Sense: hearing | Taste: sweet

Now what about the fifth sense, the touch? It transcends all seasons.

The art of pairing

Pairing and cooking follow the same rules and principles. The whisky chosen for pairing will also work well if added to the dish. The recipes presented in my book include whisky as a seasoning ingredient. You may prefer to perform the whisky pairing only. So pour the whisky in your glass instead of in the pan and enjoy!

Pairing whisky and food is all about finding harmony and balance. Choosing the appropriate whiskies to match dishes requires exactly the same efforts as with wine. You need to have some knowledge about the drink. The rest is practise and a question of taste and sensitivity as the technique is entirely based on sensory evaluation. I know that some people have tried a scientific approach, basing their pairings on chemistry, looking for similar molecular profiles but I am not convinced. For me, the appreciation of flavours goes far beyond chemistry. You can't leave out personal tastes nor cultural environment, not even your mood of the day.

Let's have a look at the whiskies first. The fantastic wheel of aromas displayed by single malts, pot-still whiskeys, bourbons or rye whiskeys generates just as many descriptives as wine does (maybe more!). It makes sense to offer one's dram a wider source of enjoyment than just aperitif or after-dinner. Tasters' notes can often be read as a full menu. A lot of sensations, whether at nosing or at tasting, are related to food. What about 'kippers', 'oxtail broth', 'peppered mackerel', 'bacon', 'crème brûlée', 'lemon meringue pie'? A rich whisky reveals itself as a 'liquid' dish !
All these obvious connections between food and whisky naturally ask for matching. Taken individually, a whisky and a dish have their own richness and character. When (well) matched, they create additional character, bringing in new flavours. One plus one equals three, not two, an odd mathematics formula I admit but so true.

Serving whisky with a meal is not just having your favourite dram with your favourite dish. If you drink a highly peated single malt, say an Octomore, alongside with a red fruit pavlova, you will not appreciate either of them. It is like wearing a red dress with an orange scarf and purple shoes. Not the best demonstration of elegance and taste.

Matching food and drinks follows simple but basic rules. It is important to note the key aromas in the whisky profile first. Either based on complementing or contrasting, pairing will then look for the 'bridge' which will make the two have a conversa-

tion. It does not have to be the main flavour. It will rather be a herb, a spice, a fruit... Then, you think of dishes which could echo or complement the aromatic palette. The importance is to keep the balance so that one does not overwhelm the other.

You can also play contrast : sweet against bitter or sour, smooth against crisp. That last suggestion implies to consider the texture. A satin-like feel will pair with a creamy sauce if you want to put the stress on smoothness. But you can also contrast that satin-like texture with a crunchy dish to make it better stand out (raw vegetables, thin slices of toasted bread).

Complementing or contrasting but avoid clashing

Many malt lovers tend to associate smoked food to peaty single malts. This is not an inspired choice as one smokiness conflicts with the other and overpowers the dish. It is better to go for a honeyed and malty whisky.

The A to Z list of the best ingredients for whisky pairing

There is no contraindication when it comes to pair whisky and food. Well, except with one ingredient: garlic, as the introductory page of the book points out. It may be read as a joke but it is not. The pungent and overwhelming taste of garlic takes possession of your taste buds and totally perverts the flavours of the whisky, no matter how powerful and characterful it is. This is why I have banned garlic from my cooking. This always comes as a surprise as people expect that, as a French born palate, I should thrive on garlic, which is, incidentally, a cliché as deeply carved in mind as the Frenchman in a beret with a baguette under his arm. In Normandy where I was born and grew up, garlic is hardly used in cooking, apart from with the ritual Easter leg of lamb. So exit garlic, but there are plenty of ingredients that whisky likes and vice-versa. Here is a list which confronts the 'do's and don'ts' as a recommendation of what to do and what to avoid when using the listed ingredient. The list is far from being exhaustive. It is up to everyone to make their own, according to their likings and where they live.

Apricot

An interesting fruit which offers a large array of matching when in season, ripe and juicy, as well as when dried. It offers a good balance between sweet and tangy flavours.

Do > Serve apricot (and custard) pie with Speyside malts such as Glenlivet, Longmorn, or Glenlossie.

Don't > Match an apricot based dish with an oaky malt, the sourness of the fruit clashes with the bitter edge of the whisky.

Cheese

A whole laboratory for your experiments. Cheese and whisky is one of the most successful duos (see the recipes p. 90).

Do > Pair a blue cheese with a peated whisky, for instance Lagavulin and Lanark Blue (with a toasted slice of 'pain de campagne' and a stick of celery as the bridge).

Don't > Present one single whisky with an assortment of cheeses, which would include a cheddar as well as a goat cheese and a blue cheese. The harmony can't be achieved. Select cheeses from a same family.

Chocolate

Obviously the most commonly practiced marriage. But again, not any chocolate will harmoniously pair with any whisky. Milk chocolate and praliné find a good match with bourbon matured whiskies.

Do > Keep dark chocolate for rich, deep, older whiskies matured in sherry casks. Orange peel, cinnamon will make perfect bridges. Get a dark chocolate with the highest cocoa content you can find and grate two tablespoons over a braised duck breast, venison, or fillet of beef. Wonderful with a Glenfarclas, a Glendronach or a Dalmore.

Don't > I personally am not a fan of mint chocolate with whisky. The mint and the crystallized sugar mixed with the chocolate cloy on the palate and make the whisky heavier or even overwhelms it.

Custard

Many malts matured in ex-bourbon casks reveal a custardy creaminess on the nose as well as on the palate. They ideally complement custard, or any savory cream sauces.

Do > Take example of the traditional 'floating island', the lightest of puddings that you can adapt to different whiskies just by flavoring the custard. With coffee, marry it to Glenrothes 1985; with orange zest, prefer Aberlour 18 Year Old and with coconut, go for Auchentoshan Classic.

Don't > Add whisky to plain custard. I always find it sickly. Cognac and rum work better than whisky.

Dried fruit

The friends of whisky are… nuts!

Do > Almond for younger whiskies, toasted hazelnuts for older ones and walnuts for old timers (especially sherried ones).

Don't > No real possibility to go wrong.

Duck

This fat, rich, tasty meat is the perfect companion of sherried whiskies such as Aberlour a'bunadh, Mortlach, or Bowmore Darkest.

Do > Add flavour to a 'duck à l'orange' with Bowmore Darkest. For best result, use an injector, which will get the whisky (that can be mixed with some clear honey) to the centre of the duck meat much quicker than any marinade.

Don't > Try to pair duck with a light floral single malt. Its flavours would completely disappear!

Garlic

Do > No way.

Don't > Garlic is said to kill vampires. It does the same for whisky (am I repeating myself here?).

Langoustines

Shellfish can be exquisite with whisky. Two great pairings: either with a peaty/iodinic malt or with a bourbon cask matured one, with a sweet vanilla profile.

Do> If you pan-fry langoustines, deglaze the pan with a good dash of whisky, a pinch of ginger and a few drops of lime juice.

Don't > Marinate the langoustines in whisky before cooking. It would burn the flesh and make it soggy.

Mushrooms

They are the perfect option for an autumnal or wintery dish. Their earthy character and their versatile use offer a large spectrum of possibilities. They especially marry well with sherried and oaky whiskies.

Do > Marinate the mushrooms 10 minutes in whisky before pan frying them.

Don't > Let them marinate too long, they would become soggy.

Onions

Cooked onions, especially when caramelized (in chutneys, sauces or salads) are a good pairing ingredient. Raw onions are too pungent and will leave a taste in your palate which will clash with whisky.

Do > Use an onion marmalade cooked in pomegranate juice with cheese or cold meat. Good match with malty whiskies.

Don't > Try to match whisky with a salad which includes raw onions. Their pungent taste will kill any whisky.

Oysters

What a great combination!

Do > Add two drops of Laphroaig in a fleshy oyster. You will hear the roaring of the sea!

Don't > It is an error to keep the first juice of the oysters once opened. Throw it and they will release another, less salty.

Pears

Young Speysiders, Lowland malts, Irish whiskeys go well with pears, either fresh and juicy or poached in a flavoured syrup.

Do > Serve pears with blue cheese and whisky (Dalwhinnie 15 Year Old) or an Irish whiskey (Tyrconnell).

Don't > No contraindication with pears. Just adapt the recipe. With a sherried whisky, poach the pears in port and spices.

Salad

Salad may not seem the obvious ingredient to match with whisky. Yet, lamb's lettuce with its distinctive texture and watercress with its spiciness both work very well.

Do > Use your salad as a 'platform' to display other ingredients: smoked fish with grassy whiskies, smoked meat with earthy ones, not hesitating to add Summer fruit or citrus fruit in the first case, apple, prunes and walnut in the second one.

Don't > Avoid drowning the salad in dressing and do not use much vinegar.

Smoked salmon

Another commonly practiced marriage.

Do > Add lemon and dill on the salmon. Excellent bridges with the whisky.

Don't > Pair smoked salmon with a smoky whisky. They totally clash.

Spices

They will echo whiskies marked by oaky notes. Or they can be used in opposition to tone down a very sweet whisky.

Do > Combine cinnamon with ginger and nutmeg and use the mix in a rice pudding or in a savoury dish such as lamb tagine.

Don't > Overcook the spices, they tend to lose their flavours. Use chili too generously, it might overwhelm the whisky.

Vegetables

The sweetness and smooth texture of root vegetables such as carrots, parsnips, Jerusalem artichokes, turnips and cucurbitaceae make an easy match with whisky.

Do > When you have roasted root vegetables in the oven, add a dash of whisky in the bottom of the dish and stir before serving or spray whisky on them.

If you serve mashed turnips or parsnips, add a handful of crushed toasted hazelnuts. Another great bridge with the whisky.

Don't > I can't see any reason to go wrong with any root vegetables.

Vinegar

You would think vinegar has to be banned. No, it can be an excellent enhancer but it has to be handled carefully.

Do > Use balsamic vinegar, it is less sour and offers an interesting aromatic range (from the youngest to the oldest).

Don't > Avoid uncooked vinegar. When cooked in a sauce though, it loses some of its tang, especially when sweetened by honey or dried fruit.

The art of cooking

Cooking with whisky is much more than about just adding any whisky to any dish. As with pairing a dram to accompany your food, cooking requires flavours as well as texture to be matched, and it works on the same aromatic scale. Just as important as a good balance of flavours – if not more so – is the way whisky is incorporated into the food. The aim is to retain the aromas while allowing the alcohol to evaporate.

I have developed a method, based on simple but precise principles during my twenty odd years of experimenting with whisky in cooking.

Avoid combining a whole spectrum of flavours. I always work in a triangular dimension: one main ingredient (whether it be meat, fish, salad, fruit etc..) and two minor ones acting in contrast, fusion or complementing.

Just as with pairing food and whisky, **find a 'bridge' between the whisky and the food,** a 'hyphen' which will facilitate the matching because it enhances a common point. It can be a condiment, a spice, or a bigger ingredient. A common denominator in fact.

Stick to the season. Forget stews in summer or strawberries in winter. And choose your whisky accordingly as, even within the range of a single distillery, there is a seasonal profile in whiskies

Treat whisky as a seasoning ingredient, just like herbs and spices. As for the amount of whisky to be used in the recipe, that depends on its aromatic profile, which is why single malts work better in cooking than blended whiskies. You can be quite generous with a light and delicate malt, whereas a heavily peated or sherried one will only need a splash. It's really a matter of chemistry but then that applies to all kinds of ingredients in cooking, n'est-ce pas?

Fish and shellfish

The key-word is freshness. This is why young vibrant bourbon cask matured whiskies will feature best. For fish, unpeated whiskies are better, for instance a Speysider like Glenfiddich 12 Year Old or Glenlivet Nàdurra will match whit fish in a creamy sauce. Non peated Highlanders such as Old Pulteney 12 Year Old or Oban 14 Year Old will go well with smoked fish or oily fishes. Smoky island whiskies will pair with oysters, mussels or lobsters. The perfect tip: a few drops of Laphroaig 10 Year Old on an oyster. Caol Ila, with its vanilla profile, pairs well with langoustines or lobster.

As with scallops, it depends how they are prepared : Bruichladdich Islay Barley with a 'surf and turf' combination such as scallops and black pudding, Isle of Jura 16 Year Old if scallops are pan-fried with mushrooms. For scallops served with butter, ginger and lemon sauce, any bourbon matured whisky will shine through (Auchentoshan American wood, The Laddie Ten, Glenmorangie 10).

Meat

There is a large spectrum of meat dishes. To sum up, beef and venison wil pair well with sherried matured whiskies. Oaky notes will go well with spicy and wine sauces. Dried fruit in the sauce or the stuffing can be a good bridge. Fruit like oranges are perfect too with duck in a salad and then, peated whiskies will find a good connection with citrus fruit.

For a roasted breast of duck and an orange sauce, go for a sherry cask matured whisky such as Glenfarclas 15 Year Old, Mortlach 15 Year Old (G & McP) or Glenrothes 1988. But depending on the type of meat, bourbon cask matured malts can also be chosen for poultry or lamb cooked with dried fruit. For instance, Glenmorangie Nectar d'Or or Glenmorangie 18 Year Old will make a scrumptious match with an apricot and almond lamb tagine, Benromach 10 Year Old with roasted pork fillet and prunes. Spicy dishes such as a 'steak au poivre' go beautifully with Talisker Storm for example.

Vegetables

The 'king' vegetable with whisky is a root vegetable - parsnips, carrots, Jerusalem artichokes, neeps, celeriac - because of its sweetness. Chestnuts used as vegetables (a soup or a purée) feature very well too. Beetroots with their earthy flavours marry with sherried whiskies. Cucurbitaceae are also on the list of the favourite vegetables. Squash and pumpkins, with their rich smooth texture and their sweet taste allow interesting combinations, especially when seasoned with exotic spices or with vanilla (cream of butternut squash and coconut milk paired with a bourbon cask matured malt).

Potatoes are a 'base' and thus, rather neutral. If they are seasoned with herbs, spices, fruit or nuts, they offer a wider range of possibilities. Raw crunchy vegetables (carrots, fennel, radishes, celery) are interesting texture wise but also taste wise (fennel and bourbon matured whiskies make a refreshing combination, agreeing on aniseed flavours).

Cheese

Cheese is probably the easiest pairing to start with. The most important is to work with one type of cheese only. Forget about serving an assortment of cheeses unless you are ready to open as many bottles of whisky as the number of cheeses you offer! It is impossible to find a consensual whisky. So here are some suggestions with one type only. With blue cheeses, go for a peated whisky (Lagavulin and roquefort make a winning pair). Cheddar wants a smooth and sweet whisky, so choose a single grain whisky or a first fill bourbon matured single malt (such as Hedonism or Glenrothes Alba Reserve). Matured cheeses (comté, gouda, gruyère) will like a malty whisky with a honeyed and fruity profile (Balvenie Double Wood, Aberlour 16 Year Old, Highland Park 12 Year Old). The more mature the cheese is, the older the whisky will be. That may sound a little extravagant but a Glenfarclas 40 Year Old and a very old gouda, salty and crumbly makes one of the best combinations I have ever tried.

Chocolate

This is probably the favorite ingredient in whisky pairing. Here again, it does not mean that any chocolate pairs with any whisky. The darker, the better with oaky and sherried whiskies. Praline, milk or white chocolate will suit creamy bourbon matured whiskies. A chocolate with a hint of salt will make a good match with a smoky whisky. The textures should also be considered : smooth chocolate fondant, light aerial mousse, crunchy icing... A chocolate fondant (semi-bitter) served with a salty caramel sauce would pair well with Bowmore 12 Year Old. Try a white chocolate cheesecake with raspberries and Glenlivet Founder's reserve. A dark chocolate tart (nuts welcome) would marry with Dalmore 15 Year Old or Lagavulin Distillers'Edition.

Other desserts

You will generally find a good connection between Speyside malts and fruit, especially pears and apples or peaches and apricots. Rhubarb is a bit more tricky because of the sour tinge of the fruit which can be challenged by icecream, honey, maple syrup or crystallised ginger.

Many malts matured in ex-bourbon casks reveal a custardy creaminess on the nose as well as on the palate. They will flatter custard if added to an accompaniment (fruit, cake, etc). The floating island for instance is a delicious pudding that you can adapt to different whiskies just by flavoring the custard (see above). It is difficult to go wrong when pairing desserts and whisky. If you opt for adding the whisky in the recipe, be light on the whisky. It is very important not to taste the alcohol.

About the techniques

Flambé
A categorical Don't !
The old cooking school in France was very fond of 'flambé', considering that the flame took the alcohol away, just to keep the flavours of the cognac the chef was using. Well... no. While the flame does burn off the alcohol, it also takes away most of the aromas. This may be fine as a piece of showmanship, but it is a waste of time and of money.

Marinating
This is an excellent way to impart whisky flavours to raw ingredients, bearing in mind that, after 15 minutes, alcohol tends to cook the fish or meat and gives it a greyish colour. Whisky will act as a meat tenderizer, but may break down the meat fibres if used to excess, and could make a steak, for example, unacceptably spongy.
Do > Marinate raw langoustines for ten minutes in lime juice, add 2 tablespoons of peated whisky (such as Caol Ila), a teaspoon of grated ginger root, grated lime and a pinch of chili. Then cook them in a pan with a touch of olive oil. Deglaze the pan at the very end with the marinade.
Don't > Soak raw salmon slices (or smoked salmon) in whisky to make a carpaccio for example.

Deglazing
As explained above, whisky can be used to deglaze a hot pan. This is the way to gather the pan juices. The pan must be very hot so that the operation can be done off the heat. A spoonful of cream or a large knob of butter will make a delicious sauce. For a sweet, why not add a spoonful of maple syrup. Always use a wooden spatula to remove all the juices from the pan. Whisky is then used as the finishing touch. Always pour the whisky right at the last minute, away from the heat.
Do > After having pan-fried pork chops, deglaze the pan off the heat with a Highland malt (such as Old Pulteney 12 Year Old) and add three tablespoons of organic apple juice. Stir energetically to take the juices off and put back on the hob 30 seconds to thicken the sauce.
Don't > Pour a large amount of whisky in the pan and let evaporate, cooking on a high heat.

Brushing
This is more a tip than a technique but it works very well, especially for cakes. Or pan-fried meats and fishes. It is very easy. Just soak the brush in the whisky. Brush the surface of the cooked food.
Do > To make a lemon drizzle cake shine, mix the whisky with a lemony syrup and brush the cake. You can poke the surface of the cake with a knife so that the whisky and the syrup penetrate better. For a barbecued leg of lamb, brush the meat with a mix of honey and whisky.
Don't > Use a high strength whisky as the alcohol will not evaporate quickly enough.

Spraying
I always have an atomizer filled with a smoky whisky by my hob. Very important: always do that at the last minute as the fragrances are evanescent.
Do > Spray a peated whisky over a cream of parsnips and toasted almonds. Do the same over a summer fruit salad.
Don't > I can't think of a don't really! I would even try this with a hot chocolate (and a sherried whisky such as Macallan or Glenfarclas).

HOW TO READ THE RECIPES

Each recipe includes the use of whisky which is treated as a seasoning ingredient, like a herb or a spice. You may choose not to add whisky to the dish and to simply pair it with one of the whiskies suggested for each recipe. However, I would recommend that you experiment with the addition of whisky. You will be amazed at how much it contributes to the flavours.

The proportions
Each recipe will serve six persons.

Weight, volume and temperature
The quantities (weight, volumes) are given in grams and millilitres and the temperatures in Celsius but tables of conversion can be found for British and American measures at the end of the book p. 156.

The whisky
To help choosing the right 'whisky to match', a short description presents the ideal profile, followed by a suggestion of five whiskies that would pair perfectly.
It is important to note that the name or the brand is not sufficient. It has to be a particular whisky with a specific maturation, age and characteristics.
If you take Aberlour single malt for instance, not all versions would fit the recipe. There is a great difference between Aberlour 10 Year Old and Aberlour a'bunadh for example.
When blended whiskies or Irish pot-stills or bourbons are given as suggestion, I use the word 'whisky' in the recipe.
When all suggestions comprise single malts, I use the word 'single malt' in the list of ingredients and method.
I found it interesting to give worldwide whiskies suggestions as whisky lovers tend more and more to venture in new territories. This said, Scottish single malts keep the pole position.

Specific ingredients

I like to use specific spices and seasonings which are common in France. Explanations and information on where to find them are given p. 159.

The season

A logo has been included by the heading as a reminder of the season.

- Spring
- Summer
- Autumn
- Winter

The sensory strip

At the top of the page, a 'sensory strip' consisting of four photos illustrates the atmosphere of the dish and the whisky that will be served with it and used in cooking, alluding to texture, colour, and seasonality.

STARTER

Raisins and carrot salad with a malty orange sauce

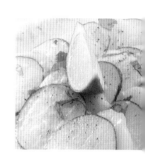

STARTERS

Salmon mousse profiteroles

Create a surprise with these light and refreshing profiteroles. They can also be served as canapés for parties or pre-dinner drinks.

For the profiteroles (3 per person)
125ml water
50g salted butter
60g plain flour
2 eggs
pinch of ground black pepper
For the stuffing
200g ricotta cheese
200g fresh raw Scottish salmon
150g smoked Scottish salmon
2tbsp single malt
1 lime (finely grated zest and juice)
2tbsp finely chopped dill
2 celery sticks (cut in very small dice)
sprigs of dill for decoration
For the sauce
3 tbsp double cream
juice of half a lemon
1 tbsp single malt
salt and ground black pepper

Preheat the oven (220°C - Gas mark 7).
Make the profiteroles. Put the water, butter and black pepper into a pan and bring to the boil until the butter is melted. Off the heat, add the flour all at once and stir vigorously. You should get a thick and compact dough that leaves the sides of the pan. Put back on the heat just to dry off the dough for a few seconds. Take off the heat again, add the eggs, one by one, continuing to beat well. The dough should be soft. Spoon 18 small profiteroles on to a baking sheet lined with greaseproof paper. Bake in the oven for 15 minutes.

Make the mousse. Dice both the salmons into tiny cubes. In a bowl, mix together all the other ingredients of the stuffing. Season with salt and pepper. Add the salmon, stir well. Cut each profiterole in two and stuff them with this mixture. To make the sauce, mix all the listed ingredients together.
Place 3 profiteroles on each plate. Garnish with a drizzle of sauce. Decorate with dill.

WHISKIES TO MATCH

PROFILE
A young or NAS (non age statement) single malt matured in bourbon cask which will be served chilled.

SUGGESTIONS
The Glenlivet Founder Reserve
Mackmyra Bruks
Auchentoschan Classic
Glenrothes Alba Reserve
Glenmorangie 10 Year Old

Whisky flavoured minty green pea velouté

A chilled soup, yes ... not the usual Vichyssoise but, this time, a very bright green pea delicacy refreshed by mint and harmoniously laced with whisky. A must for a light Spring first course.

500g frozen green peas
600ml vegetable consommé
150ml whipping cream
3 mint stems
3 tbsp single malt
salt, ground black pepper

Bring 2 litres of salted water to the boil. Then add the green peas and cook for 8 minutes. Drain and place immediately into iced water for a few seconds. Drain well.

Set aside 6 leaves of mint. Roughly chop the remaining mint leaves, bring the cream to the boil, add the mint leaves. Take off the heat, leave to infuse for 10 minutes and then strain. Allow the cream to cool.

Bring the vegetable consommé to the boil. Add the cooked peas. Check the seasoning. Heat for 4 minutes. Using an electric blender, blend until the texture is smooth. Divide into six bowls and put in the fridge to chill.

Whip the mint infused cream with the single malt and top each bowl with it before serving. Serve with a toasted brioche and a herb butter (see p. 140).

FLAVOUR TIP

Seafood can be added to accompany this delicate soup. Mix sesame oil, lemon juice, 2 tbsp of single malt, allspice and cayenne pepper. Pour over prawns (scallops or langoustines). Leave to marinate for 20 minutes. Before serving, warm a non stick pan and sear the seafood with the marinade 2 to 3 minutes until all liquid is evaporated. Skewer a mint leaf and a prawn on a cocktail stick. Season with cayenne pepper and place on the bowl.

WHISKIES TO MATCH

PROFILE

Combined with the soft pink shade of the prawns, this quite simple soup calls for a delicate yet complex single malt. Either floral, grassy or fruity, it needs to be silky, light and firm.

SUGGESTIONS

Aberlour 10 Year Old
Bruichladdich The Laddie 10 Year Old
Caol Ila Moch
Arran 10 Year Old
anCnoc 12 Year Old

Scottish Sushi

These sushi should be called makis but I like the name sushi better! Makis are usually rolled in a nori (seaweed) leaf. To be Scottish, it has to be salmon and the rice is replaced by pearl barley while horseradish is the alternative for wasabi.

For 18 sushi
150g smoked salmon (6 large slices)
4 tbsp pearl barley (cooked)
2 tbsp horseradish sauce
3 tbsp cream cheese (or ricotta)
1tsp fresh coriander (chopped)
plus some leaves for decoration
1/2 avocado
the juice of half a lemon
ground black pepper
Sauce
3 tbsp horseradish sauce
1 tbsp rice vinegar
1 pinch ground ginger
1 tbsp whisky

Cut the smoked salmon into regular strips (about 2,5cm x 10cm). Cut the half avocado in sticks of the same length. Pour the lemon juice over the avocado to avoid it turning black.
Mix all the other ingredients in a bowl.
Place a teaspoon of the mixture on a salmon strip, leaving a space of 1cm from the edge. Place an avocado stick in the center. Roll the salmon onto itself over the barley mixture to obtain a cylinder.
Add a coriander leaf to decorate.
Mix all the ingredients for the sauce and serve in small dishes so that people can dip the sushi in it.
Spray whisky on the sushi before serving.

THE SMART TIP
For vegetarians, replace the salmon with a paper thin strip of courgette, quickly blanched and pat dried with kitchen paper so that it becomes supple enough to roll it without breaking. Also, make sure the cheese you use is suitable for vegetarians.

WHISKIES TO MATCH

PROFILE
Non peated malts ou blended whiskies, mostly matured in bourbon casks, rather young.

SUGGESTIONS
Auchentoshan Classic
Hakushu 12 Year Old
Hibiki Harmony
Glencadam 10 Year old
Glen Grant 10 Year Old

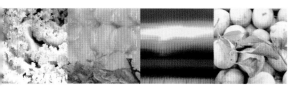

Carpaccio of scallops
with crunchy vegetables and crab salad

Serving raw scallops is a little intimidating as you never know if your guests will like it. Here, surrounded by crab and crunchy vegetables, they look so appetizing that everyone will crave them.

18 raw scallops (trimmed and cleaned)
without their roe
200g white crab meat
2 limes
10 radishes
2 tbsp fresh coriander (finely chopped)
3 tbsp olive oil
2 tbsp truffle oil
fleur de sel
ground black pepper
thin slices of black truffles (optional)

Grate the zest of one lime, squeeze the lime and mix the juice and the zest. Blend the two oils with the lime juice and zest, season. Pour half of it on the crab and mix.

Carefully slice each scallop into 3 slices. Slice the radishes as finely as possible.

To serve: spoon a line of crab salad on either side of rectangular dinner plates. At the centre, alternate scallop and radishes. Brush the scallops with the rest of the lime dressing. Season with fleur de sel and ground pepper.
Sprinkle with coriander. Add the truffle shavings (optional).
Cut the second lime into small wedges and use to garnish the dish.

THE 'PLUS' TIP
Give a light spray with one of the single malts suggested onto each dinner plate, just before serving.

WHISKIES TO MATCH

PROFILE
Light and smooth malts, peated (if so, choose a lightly peated whisky) or non peated. A spicy touch is welcome

SUGGESTIONS
Ardbeg Blasda
Aultmore 12 Year Old
Glann ar Mor Maris Otter Barley
Glenfiddich 12 Year Old
Clynelish 14 year Old

Scallops & black pudding Surf & Turf with apple sauce

The initial reaction would be that the strong flavour of black pudding might overwhelm the delicacy of the scallop. Not at all. The combination is amazing, provided the right whisky is chosen to pair with.

12 big scallops
4 slices of Stornoway black pudding
30g salted butter
250ml apple juice (or cider)
1 tbsp cider vinegar
1 tbsp olive oil
1 large Bramley apple, cooked and puréed
1 pinch of cinnamon
3 tbsp whisky
salt, ground black pepper
sprigs of chervil

Crumble the black pudding onto a hot non-stick pan for a few minutes until the crumbs are dry and firm. Reserve on a warm plate. Keep the same pan for cooking the scallops, making sure you remove any excess fat from the black pudding. Season the scallops on both sides. Melt the butter with olive oil and sear the scallops, one minute on each side. Reserve on a warm plate (with the black pudding).

Deglaze the pan with the cider vinegar then add the apple juice. Add the apple purée and the cinnamon, and stir well to absorb all the cooking juices. Leave to reduce for 5 minutes on a high heat. Add the whisky one minute before the end.

To serve : place the scallops on each individual warm dinner plate, spoon the black pudding crumbs on top.
Quickly strain the sauce and spoon around the scallops. Decorate with sprigs of chervil.

FLAVOUR TIP
If you wish to serve a vegetable with this dish may I suggest that you lay the scallops on a bed of pureed green pea and brocoli previously spooned at the centre of each plate.

WHISKIES TO MATCH

PROFILE
Peat and spice pairs well with black pudding. But a malty/grassy core is needed to 'converse' with the scallops. So, characterful but with a sweet heart.

SUGGESTIONS
Kornog Saint-Yvy 2014
Old Pulteney 17 Year Old
Yoichi 10 Year Old
The Peat Monster
Craigellachie 17 Year Old

Raisins and carrot salad with a malty orange sauce

Easy, straightforward, light and appetizing, this salad with a Moroccan touch encapsulates the vivid cheerfulness of Summer.

300g carrots
3 tbsp raisins
4 tbsp whisky
2 tbsp walnut oil
2 tbsp grape seed oil
1 tbsp malt vinegar
the juice of an orange
1 tbsp grated orange zest
1 tbsp coconut shavings
2 tbsp chopped fresh coriander
ground black pepper
fleur de sel
4 tbsp whisky

Soak the raisins in 3 tablespoons of whisky and then heat gently in the microwave for 20 seconds or over low heat in a pan on the hob. Leave to infuse for 30 minutes.

Peel the carrots and grate them finely. Mix both oils, vinegar, orange juice and zest and the last spoonful of whisky in a bowl. Add fleur de sel and ground black pepper to taste.

Place the grated carrots in a large bowl, add raisins soaked in whisky. Pour the dressing over the carrots. Mix thoroughly. Sprinkle with coriander and shavings. Chill in the fridge until serving.

FLAVOUR TIP

Warming the raisins and whisky for few seconds helps the whisky to penetrate so that the fruit swells quicker. To enhance the coconut flavour in the dressing, you can replace 2 tablespoons of grape seed oil by the same quantity of coconut milk. A touch of ground ginger or cinnamon brings out the flavours.

WHISKIES TO MATCH

PROFILE
A sherried whisky for the fruit harmony or a bourbon if the emphasis is put on the coconut in the recipe.

SUGGESTIONS
The GlenDronach 12 Year Old
The Macallan Amber
Highland Park 12 Year Old
Mortlach 15 Year Old (Gordon & MacPhail)
Maker's Mark

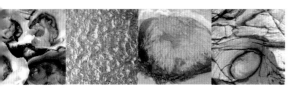

Oysters in a seajelly

Oysters are the perfect companion for smoky and seaweedy single malts. The simpler, the better. The main point is not to shuck the oysters until the stage indicated in the recipe

18 big oysters
3 gelatine leaves
2 branches of dill (finely chopped)
3 tbsp single malt
ground black pepper

Open the oysters, transfer the shell liquid into a bowl. Wait a little until the oysters naturally release a second amount of liquid. Transfer it again in the same bowl. Proceed immediately to the preparation of the jelly, and only shuck the oysters while the jelly sets.

Soak the gelatine leaves in cold water for 10 minutes. Strain the oysters' seawater from the bowl into a saucepan and bring to the boil. Leave to cool a little and add the drained and squeezed gelatine leaves. Stir until the gelatine is melted. Add the single malt. When the jelly starts to set, pour it into the oyster shells. Season with ground black pepper. Top each shell with one oyster and pour the rest of the jelly over the oysters.

Sprinkle with dill and leave in the fridge to set completely.

THE FRENCH WAY

Oysters which, like in some Western restaurants, arrive in front of you already shucked may not be always safe for consumption, as you have no way of checking how long they have been standing like this in their shells. In France, we never shuck oysters for that very reason.

Also, when you eat fresh oysters in their raw state, it is important to discard the first shell juices, simply by turning them upside down. A very fresh oyster will immediately release a second amount of liquid which is less briny and more in harmony with the delicate flavours of the oyster.

THE FLAVOUR TIP

Just spray your oyster with a peated single or blended malt (see below). This would replace lemon, tabasco or any other accompaniment.

WHISKIES TO MATCH

PROFILE
Definitely peated malts.

SUGGESTIONS
Big Peat
Laphroaig 10 Year Old (40% or cask strength)
Connemara
Chichibu The Peated
Ardbeg Perpetuum

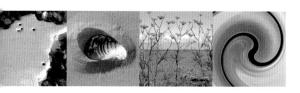

Mussels and shrimp crumble with a whisky jus

Crumble does not have to be just a sweet dish. This savoury version brings in a lovely crunchy texture to the dish and reveals the delights of seafood under its crust.

1 fennel bulb
2 medium white onions
80g butter
100ml dry vermouth (or white wine)
1 lime (grated zest and juice)
150g shelled prawns
1kg mussels
2 tbsp chopped parsley
3 tbsp whisky
salt, ground black pepper
For the crumble
100g plain flour
50g oatmeal
80g chopped hazelnuts (lightly toasted)
120g salted butter
ground black pepper

Raise the oven heat to 200°C (gas marked 6).

Place the mussels in a pan and heat for a few minutes until all the mussels are open. Remove from the heat, shell them and keep warm. Strain the cooking juices and reserve.

Slice the fennel and the onions into thin slices. Melt 50g butter in a pan. Add the onions and fennel. Simmer for a few minutes, add the vermouth and the mussel cooking juice plus a small glass of water if needed. Taste and season with black pepper. Cook for 10 minutes on low heat until the liquid has reduced by 2/3. Spoon into an ovenproof dish (or individual dishes).

Make the crumble. Preheat the oven (180°C - Gas mark 4). In a bowl, mix all the dry ingredients and add butter bit by bit. Rub in until you have a 'crumbly' texture. Sprinkle onto a baking sheet lined with greaseproof paper and bake for 10 minutes in the oven.

Melt the rest of the butter in the pan and seal the prawns for a few minutes. Add the lime zest and juice. Deglaze with the whisky. Place the mussels and shrimps on top of the fennel. Then cover with the crumble. Bake for 8 minutes (200°C - Gas mark 6).

WHISKIES TO MATCH

PROFILE
Whiskies with a malty and 'pâtissier' profile (to match with the buttery crumble). Mostly bourbon matured malt or grain whiskies, with an enticing complexity.

SUGGESTIONS
The Glenfiddich Solera Reserve 14 Year Old
Glenkinchie 12 Year Old
Jameson 12 Year Old
Hedonism
Writer's tears

Salad of marinated mushrooms and smoked duck magret

Mushrooms epitomize that colourful and charming season that is autumn. The fragrances of humus and undergrowth and the tawny and orangy colours of this simple salad call for a cosy friendly gathering round a logfire.

A choice of green leaves
12 chestnut mushrooms
the juice and zest of an orange plus
6 orange segments
40g walnuts, chopped
18 thin slices of smoked duck magret
For the vinaigrette
2 tbsp walnut oil
2 tbsp grape seed oil
1 tbsp sherry vinegar
2 tbsp single malt
1 tsp honey
the remaining liquid from the marinade

Remove the stem of the mushrooms and discard. Wash and slice the mushrooms. Marinade the mushrooms for 15 minutes in the orange juice and zest. Season with salt and pepper.

Divide the green leaves between 6 plates. Make the vinaigrette by mixing all the ingredients listed. Spoon over the salad. Sprinkle with the walnuts. Top with the mushrooms and the duck magret. Finish with an orange segment.

FLAVOUR TIP

Feeling extravagant? If you can afford it and if you know where to find it, replace the mushrooms with a black truffle. The flavours are amazing!
Another more affordable tip: sprinkle toasted gingerbread on the salad.

WHISKIES TO MATCH

PROFILE
Two options (or a combined one) : sherried single malts (for the duck magret) or peated ones (for the orange) but in this case, replace the smoked magret by unsmoked one.

SUGGESTIONS
Ardbeg Uigeadail
Dalmore 15 Year Old
Glenfarclas 15 Year Old
Bunnahabhain 18 Year Old
Highland Park - Dark Origins

Velouté of roasted butternut squash and coconut

Pumpkins, marrows, squashes are another emblematic autumn vegetable. And, if it is the dish of Halloween par excellence, all cucurbitaceae are now seen as the comforting colourful vegetables of chillier months.

600g butternut squash
2 tbsp olive oil
250ml coconut milk
150ml double cream
2 tbsp whisky
3 tbsp toasted almonds
1 pinch Espelette chili
fleur de sel and ground black pepper

Peel the squash, cut in large dice, place in an ovenproof dish. Sprinkle with olive oil and chili and roast for 35 minutes in a hot oven (200°C - Gas mark 6).

Warm the coconut milk with 150 ml of water. Add the cooked butternut squash then blend until you have a smooth creamy texture. Add the chili, the fleur de sel and the pepper. Whip the cream until frothy and add whisky. Toast the almonds under the grill.

Divide the velouté between six individual soup bowls. Top with a scoop of whisky cream and sprinkle with the almonds.

FLAVOUR TIP
The butternut squash can be replaced by sweet potatoes that will also give a lovely orangy colour. The recipe will stay the same.

WHISKIES TO MATCH

PROFILE
A whisky with a satin-like texture, malty and smooth. A smoked touch will bring a flavoursome contrast to the root vegetable sweetness.

SUGGESTIONS
Kornog
The Benromach Peat Smoke
Glenmorangie Tùsail
Johnnie Walker Gold Label Reserve
Nikka White Pure Malt

Herb & citrus pain perdu
with whisky laced haddock mousse

Here is a delicious recipe to use any bread leftovers. Pain perdu is not only a dessert, it can be cooked as a savoury dish. Pain perdu translates as lost bread. It is the epitome of Cuisine Grand-mère, when all is used and nothing is wasted.

For the haddock mousse
400g smoked haddock (cooked and skinned)
2 tbsp olive oil
100g cream cheese or ricotta
the juice of a lemon
2 tbsp horseradish sauce
2 tbsp chopped chives
1 large pinch chilli
ground black pepper
For the pain perdu
6 slices of stale brioche or toasting bread
100 ml single cream
2 tbsp tarragon; 2 tbsp dill; 2 tbsp flat parsley
2 eggs
2 tbsp whisky
1 tbsp lemon zest
40g salted butter
salt & ground black pepper
sprigs of dill for decoration

Make the haddock mousse. Place all the ingredients in the blender bowl, blend to obtain a smooth mousse. Check the seasoning. Keep in the fridge.

Make the pain perdu. Cut the bread into six slices. Bring the cream to the boil. Put the herbs in a bowl and pour in the cream. Whisk to obtain a smooth emulsion. In another bowl, whisk the eggs with the lemon zest and the whisky. Season with salt and ground pepper. Pour the cream emulsion into the egg mixture. Stir well. Pour the mixture into a shallow dish.

Melt the butter in a frying pan. Quickly dip each slice of bread into the egg mixture and pan fry one at a time one minute on each side.

To serve : place a slice of pain perdu on each individual plate, shape the haddock mousse between two soup spoons and lay it on the bread. Decorate with a sprig of dill.

WHISKIES TO MATCH

PROFILE
A malty unpeated whisky, focusing on cereal and Autumn fruit (apples and pears) will be perfect. Certainly a rustic character.

SUGGESTIONS
Old Pulteney 12 Year Old
Jura Origins 10 Year Old
Glenkinchie Distillers Edition
Berry's Speyside Reserve
Lord Elcho 15 Year Old (Wemyss whiskies)

Baked figs with gingerbread
and foie gras medallion with a whisky sauce

Here is a festive recipe which could easily appear on the Christmas table. It is not always easy to find fresh figs in the middle of winter but they are worth looking for. Duck foie gras is tastier than the goose one.

12 big fresh figs
1 thick slice of gingerbread (crumbled)
30g butter
1 tbsp clear honey
1 tbsp sherry vinegar
2 tbsp single malt
1 tsp ground cardamon (6 pods, seeds toasted and crushed in a mortar)
salt, ground black pepper

For the sauce
40g foie gras (cut in dice)
1 tbsp crème fraîche
1 tbsp single malt
fleur de sel, ground black pepper

To garnish
6 thin round slices of foie gras
6 toasted gingerbread rounds
fleur de sel

Preheat the oven (210°C - Gas mark 6/7). Grease an ovenproof dish. Wash the figs, make an incision on the top, open them slightly and delicately spoon some gingerbread crumbs inside each one.
Melt the butter with the vinegar, ground cardamom and single malt. Place the figs in the ovenproof dish. Brush them with the butter mixture and pour the rest in the dish with 50ml of water. Sprinkle the rest of gingerbread over the figs. Cook 10 minutes in the oven.

Make the sauce. Place the foie gras and cream in a bowl placed over a pan of simmering water (bain-marie). Add fleur de sel and black pepper. Whisk to melt the foie gras into the cream. Take off the heat and add the single malt. Strain to obtain a smooth sauce.

Place a slice of foie gras on each gingerbread round. Place two figs on each plate. Strain the cooking juice and add it to the foie gras sauce which should be thick. Place gingerbread rounds and foie gras medallions on top of the figs. Spoon the sauce around. Sprinkle with fleur de sel.

WHISKIES TO MATCH

PROFILE
Complex single malts hence older, preferably with a finish in Port casks (perfect harmony with the figs) or PX (Pedro Ximinez).

SUGGESTIONS
The Balvenie PortWood 21 Year Old
Lagavulin Distillers Edition (PX finish)
Edradour 2003 - Port Cask Matured
The Glenlivet 18 Year Old
Tobermory 15 Year Old

Cream of lentils Cappucino with Parmesan tuiles

Lentils du Puy come from the centre of France (around the city of Le Puy). They have a particular rustic & earthy taste with a thick skin. They are the favourite lentils of many a Michelin Star chef.

Serves 6
1 bag of 500g precooked du Puy lentils
700ml of a good lamb, venison or beef stock
1 onion, finely diced
30g salted butter, 1 tbsp olive oil
100ml whipping cream
1 pinch of allspice
2 tbsp single malt
ground pepper
For the tuiles
100g finely grated Parmesan
50g grated gruyère
pinch of ground black pepper

Sauté the onion in butter and olive oil in a saucepan. Add the stock and the lentils. Season with black pepper. Simmer for 10 minutes, take off the heat then blend until thick and creamy. Keep warm on a low heat.

Preheat the oven (200°C - Gas mark 6).
Make the Parmesan tuiles. Mix the cheeses with the black pepper, then sprinkle a heaped tablespoon of cheese on a baking sheet lined with greaseproof paper to form a round of 2.5 inches (4 cm) in diameter. Bake for 3 minutes. The cheese should have melted. Remove from the oven, leave to cool for 1 minute on the baking sheet. When cool, carefully remove from the greaseproof paper and place them on to a kitchen paper to remove any excess fat. Be careful, they will be very fragile.

Whip the cream in a bowl, add allspice and the whisky while continuing to whip. Pour the lentil cream into coffee cups or glasses. Do not fill them right up, leave 2 cm at the top. Top with the whipped cream and serve with a Parmesan tuile on the side.

WHISKIES TO MATCH

PROFILE
The earthy character of the lentils match with oaky and smoky whiskies. A crisp texture with a slight oak grip will find a good harmony with the crunchy cheese tuile.

SUGGESTIONS
Aberlour 12 Year Old Double cask
Bunnahabhain 12 Year Old - Provenance - Douglas Laing
The Glenrothes 1995
Harbour Delight - 1997/2014
   (Wemyss whiskies)
Ardbeg Uigeadail

Chestnuts and foie gras velouté laced with whisky

Winter is the perfect time to think, dress, drink and eat festively. This refined soup, combined with an elegant and rich Speyside single malt, will be another royal start to a Christmas or Burns dinner.

Serves 6
250g chestnuts (cooked)
750ml beef consommé (or chicken broth)
1 tbsp mixed ground spices : cayenne pepper, white, black and cubèbe pepper, coriander seeds
4 cardamom pods (opened)
150ml double cream
4 tbsp single malt
200g foie gras (cut into small dice)
2 tbsp celery (cut into tiny dice)
1 tbsp chopped chives
salt, ground pepper

Set aside 6 chestnuts. Bring the consommé to the boil in a saucepan. Add the rest of the chestnuts. Season with salt and ground black pepper. Add the spices (the cardamom pods must be opened to release more flavours). Simmer for 10 minutes.

Take the cardamom pods out. Liquidise the soup in a blender. Pass through a sieve and keep warm on a low heat. Cut the 6 remaining chestnuts into thin slices. Sear them 5 to 6 minutes in a non stick pan until you get crunchy crisps.

Whip the cream with the single malt until it thickens. Add a pinch of ground pepper. Divide the soup into six bowls. Place the foie gras and celery dice on top. Add a quenelle of whisky cream in the middle. Sprinkle with the chestnut crisps and chopped chives.

FLAVOUR TIP
A dash of truffle juice will certainly not spoil the broth!

WHISKIES TO MATCH

PROFILE
All full-bodied Speyside malts (with a sherry touch and a slightly earthy character) will be number one choice. But you can also venture elsewhere in quest of a similar profile. That combination of rich characters result into a smooth, velvety and satisfying dish.

SUGGESTIONS
Aberlour 15 Year Old
The Balvenie Double Wood 12 Year Old
The Macallan 18 Year Old
The GlenDronach Revival 15 Year Old
Isle of Jura 16 Year Old

Old Cheddar and mushroom quiche

A main dish for an evening meal or a starter in smaller portions, this quiche is easy to prepare, tasty and always makes an impression when brought to the table.

A sheet of puff pastry
(350 x 225 mm)
100g matured cheddar
4 tbsp whisky
400g mushrooms
1 tsp coriander seeds (crushed)
1 tbsp hazelnut oil
30g unsalted butter
60ml vermouth
2 eggs plus 1 yolk
100g ricotta
100ml double cream
2 tbsp single malt

Cut 6 thin slices on the piece of cheddar, reserve for later. Cut the rest of the cheese into small dice and marinate them in the whisky for 15 minutes.

Preheat the oven (210°C - Gas mark 7). Wash the mushrooms, trim the stem and cut them into thin slices. Warm the butter and oil in a pan. Add the mushrooms and the coriander seeds. Sauté them for a few minutes then add the vermouth. Season. Simmer for 4 minutes. Drain the mushrooms and reserve the cooking juices.

In a bowl, whisk the eggs with the ricotta. Add the cream and the cooking juice from the mushrooms. Strain the diced cheddar. Add the whisky marinade to the eggs.

Roll out the puff pastry to a thickness of 2 mm and use it to line a greased quiche dish. Spread the mushrooms and the cheddar dice over the pastry. Pour the egg mixture into the dish. Top with the slices of cheddar.
Bake for 25 to 30 minutes.

FLAVOUR TIP
For extra flavour, you may add a few diced apples to the cheddar and mushrooms.

WHISKIES TO MATCH

PROFILE
A fruity, malty and complex whisky - hence rather old - will find a perfect match with the mature Cheddar. It can have a touch of sherry (but not overwhelming).

SUGGESTIONS
Aberlour 16 Year Old
Strathisla 12 Year Old
Red Breast 15 Year Old
Blanton Special reserve
Glenfiddich Rich Oak

MAIN COURSES

Spicy roasted salmon with tender cabbage and a beurre blanc nantais

A tasty fish dish with a classic sauce that I have revisited. The traditional recipe of 'beurre blanc nantais' does not include cream. But that addition makes the sauce more stable. And don't forget I am a Norman!

For the roasted salmon
6 Scottish salmon fillets (6 x 170g)
6 tbsp hazelnut oil
6 tbsp whisky
60 shelled and crushed hazelnuts
mixed spices such as : 15 cardamom pods,
20 coriander seeds, 1/2 tbsp sechouan pepper,
cubebe pepper, ground black pepper, cayenne
pepper, cumin, 3 tsp sesame seeds, one big
pinch ground cinnamon
sea-salt

For the vegetables
a small Savoy cabbage (650g)
1 tbsp sea-salt
80g unsalted butter
3 star anis, 1/2 tbsp curry powder,
1/2 tbsp allspice
salt, ground black pepper

For the sauce
3 shallots finely chopped
400ml white wine vinegar
400ml white wine
2 tbsp thick cream
150g salted butter (diced)
ground black pepper

Toast the hazelnuts in a dry frying pan with the cardamom seeds for 5 minutes. Put them in a mortar with the rest of the spices and crush them roughly.

Skin the salmon. Brush the fillets with the whisky first, then with the hazelnut oil. Spread the spices and the nuts on a plate. Roll each fish fillet into the mixture (covering both sides). Place the fillets in an oven ready dish. Set aside. Preheat the oven (240 °C - Gas mark 9).

In the meantime, blanch the cabbage into the boiling water for 1 minute. Drain and put straight into cold water. Chop the leaves into large strips. Melt half of the butter in a large saucepan, add the cabbage, salt and spices with 100 ml of water. Simmer over a low heat for 10 minutes. Add the rest of the butter and keep warm.

Place the salmon fillets in the oven and bake them for 5 minutes then reduce the heat to 180°C (Gas mark 4) and cook for 5 more minutes. While the fish is cooking, prepare the sauce. Put the shallots, the vinegar, the wine and black pepper into a pan. Bring to the boil and reduce over low heat until nearly all the liquid has evaporated. Pour the cream into the liquid,. And then, still over low heat, whisk the butter into the sauce, one small piece at a time, until the sauce has reached ribbon stage. You can also do this in a bain-marie, placing the ingredients in a bowl over a pan of simmering water.

Spoon a mound of stewed cabbage in the centre of each plate, top it with a salmon fillet, spoon the sauce around it and decorate the salmon with a sprig of chervil or flat parsley.

Chicken supreme in a lemon and tarragon sauce

The cream sauce here is enhanced by the tang of the citrus fruit and the light aniseed flavour of the tarragon while the addition of fresh ginger gives a definite kick to the final result. The combination of flavours is amazing!

6 chicken breasts
6 small onions peeled
30g butter
1tbsp olive oil
juice and zest of a lemon
100ml white wine
1tbsp grated ginger
1 tbsp grated lemon
3 tbsp chopped tarragon (2+1)
150ml chicken stock
3 tbsp crème fraîche
3 tbsp whisky
ground black pepper, salt
For the sauteed mushrooms
30g butter
450g chestnut mushrooms
1 tsp coriander seeds
ground black pepper, salt

Melt the butter with a little olive oil in a heavy-bottomed pan. When the butter starts bubbling, add the chicken breast and brown it on both sides. When the meat is browned, add the wine and the lemon juice and zest. Reduce the liquid for a few minutes then add the chicken stock, grated ginger, lemon zest and 2 tablespoons tarragon. Season with salt and pepper. Simmer gently over low heat for 25 minutes.

Wash the mushrooms, cut them into thick slices. Sauté them with oil, butter and coriander seeds for 5 minutes. Season. Add them to the chicken 5 minutes before the end of cooking.

Take the chicken and the mushrooms out of the sauce and keep in a warm serving dish. Reduce the sauce for a few minutes on the hob at a high heat, add the cream and boil for 2 min. Take off the heat and add the whisky. Stir and pour over the chicken. Sprinkle with chopped tarragon. Serve with mashed potatoes or fresh pasta.

WHISKIES TO MATCH

PROFILE

The tangy flavour of the sauce calls for a smooth and sweet whisky, malty and/or fruity. When it comes to peat, a touch of smoke is welcomed but not a marine kind of peatiness.

SUGGESTIONS

Glen Grant 16 Year Old
anCnoc 16 Year Old
Bushmills Original
Cragganmore 12 Year Old
The Malt Loaf - 2002/2014
(Wemyss whiskies)

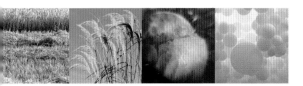

Gougère

This classic French recipe originates from Burgundy. Made of choux pastry, it can also be served in small profiteroles as an apéritif. Cooked as a large crown, it makes a delicious main dish for dinner, with a salad.

250ml water
100g salted butter
125g flour
4 eggs
ground black pepper
150g Gruyère style cheese
2 tbsp whisky

Preheat the oven (220°C - Gas mark 7). Grate 90g of cheese and dice the rest. Marinate the diced cheese in the whisky.

To make the choux pastry, put the water, the butter and black pepper in a pan and bring to the boil. Off the heat, add the flour all at once and stir vigorously with a spatula until it forms a ball of dough which comes away from the side of the saucepan. Return the pan to low heat just to dry off the dough for a few seconds. Using the spatula, work the eggs into the dough, one at a time, stirring well. The mixture must be soft. It must just fall off the spoon easily whilst still holding its shape, which means that, depending on the size of the eggs, you may use only 3 eggs. Blend in the marinated diced cheese and half the grated cheese.

Spoon the mixture in the shape of a ring onto a baking tray lined with greaseproof paper. Sprinkle the surface of the ring with the rest of the grated cheese.
Bake in the oven for 25 to 30 minutes until the gougère is puffed and golden.
You can also make individual gougères. They will take less time to cook.
Serve immediately with a green salad.

WHISKIES TO MATCH

PROFILE
Butter and cheese are the main ingredients in this dish. They will match with a 'pâtissier' whisky. A nutty touch will enhance the cheese flavours. Unpeated, malty and nutty malts will work perfectly.

SUGGESTIONS
Glen Garioch 1797 Founder's Reserve
Bruichladdich 16 Year Old - Bourbon
Cù bocan Virgin Oak
Glenmorangie Duthac
Midleton Dair Ghaelach

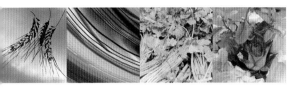

Risotto of pearl barley and spring vegetables

This is a delicious vegetarian recipe, a good alternative to an Italian risotto, say it is a Scottish risotto. The type of vegetables and spices can vary according to individual taste and season.

500g young carrots
250g frozen peas
18 green asparagus
1 tsp ground cumin
40g butter
1 tsp clear honey
40g pine kernels
For the barley
1 medium onion, chopped
40g butter, 2 tbsp olive oil
150g pearl barley
1tsp ground cumin
1 large pinch ground ginger; 1 large pinch chilli
juice of one orange (and 1 tbsp zest)
1 bunch of coriander, chopped
salt & ground black pepper
80g grated Parmesan (optional)

Clean the carrots thoroughly. Put them in a steamer basket. Sprinkle the cumin over them and steam for 10 minutes. In another pan, bring salted water to the boil and cook the aspara-gus tips and the frozen peas together for 5 to 6 minutes. Drain, keeping the vegetable water and plunge the vegetables in iced water for 10 seconds.

To cook the barley, melt the butter with some oil in a large pan. Add the spices. Fry the onions for 3 minutes, then add the pearl barley. Stir for 2 minutes and add the vegetable cooking water. Bring to a gentle simmer, cover with a lid and cook for 50 minutes. The barley must be swollen but not too soft. Keep aside.

In a frying pan, melt the remaining butter, add the carrots and, stirring constantly, add the honey until the carrots caramelize. Season to taste with salt and pepper then add the pine kernels. Stir for a few minutes. Add the chopped coriander then the peas.

Warm the barley on a low heat, add the orange juice and zest. Stir gently and add the carrots and the peas. Top with the asparagus.
Serve with grated Parmesan on the side.

— WHISKIES TO MATCH —

PROFILE
This light and fresh dish will pair with a delicate, floral whisky. Either a Lowland malt, a single grain whisky or a light Irish whiskey.

SUGGESTIONS
Jack Teeling Single Grain
Balblair 2004 - 1st release Bourbon Matured
anCnoc 12 Year Old
Tamdhu 10 Year Old - Single minded (Douglas Laing)
Mackmyra Bruks

Baked salmon and halibut in a spicy crust, served with a lemon, butter and ginger sauce

Ginger and spices give a delicious kick to these two delicate fishes and invite us to enjoy the warmth of Summer. Let the sunshine in!

400g salmon
400g halibut or sea-bass (one piece of each fish per person)
4 oatcakes, crushed
2 tbsp very finely chopped dill or chervil
40g butter
1 tbsp Sechouan pepper; 3 long peppercorns (Indonesian pepper); 1 tbsp ground black pepper; 1 tsp ground ginger
8 dried apricots finely chopped
1 tbsp lemon or lime grated zest
fleur de sel

For the sauce
500 ml good fish stock
30g fresh ginger
100g butter
Juice of lemon
1 tsp lemon grated zest

For the garnish
200g mangetout peas (steamed),
2 parsnips
60g butter
2 tbsp whisky
40g Parmesan in shavings
1 big pinch of cumin
ground black pepper, salt

The day before serving, grate the ginger and add to the fish stock. Strain and reduce the stock before use.

To prepare the crust, toast the spices in a dry frying pan and then crush them finely. Mix with the herbs, apricots, lemon zest, oatcakes and soft butter. Seal the fish in a little olive oil in the same frying pan. Then place the fish pieces on a greased oven tray. Cover each piece of fish with a thin coat of the spicy crust.

Prepare the garnish: peel the parsnips, cut them into slices and boil for 10 minutes in salted water. Drain and place the parsnips slices in a bowl. Add the whisky and spices. Mix and set aside.
Butter individual moulds. Fill with layers of parsnips and Parmesan, dotting each layer with small pieces of butter. Finish with Parmesan. Bake for 10 minutes in the oven (200°C - Gas mark 6), and then finish under the grill for 5 to 8 minutes, just before serving.

Bake the fish in the oven 8 to 10 minutes, depending on the thickness of the fillets.
To make the sauce, add lemon juice and zest to the stock and reduce again to obtain around 100ml of liquid. Then slowly whisk in the butter little by little until the sauce is thick enough to coat the back of a spoon.

On a plate, place a piece of each fish on top of mangetout peas, Remove the parsnips from the mould, tipping the mould onto the plate. Spoon a little sauce over each plate. Decorate with chervil or dill.

WHISKIES TO MATCH

PROFILE

The spice crust is the focus. A whisky with a rich spicy festoon and a sweet malty core ensures the right balance. A Highland malt, or a characterful blend.

SUGGESTIONS

Arran, The Port Cask Finish
Ben Nevis 10 Year Old
Oban 14 Year Old
Dewar's 12 Year Old
Spice King 12 Year Old (Wemyss whiskies)

Shellfish and Tartufo Risotto

This is the best of Italy on your plate! The main ingredient you need with risotto is... patience as you will be stirring your rice for 15 to 20 minutes. This is essential. But your efforts will be rewarded.

12 langoustines, 12 scallops, 500g mussels
2 tbsp whisky
1ltr of shellfish stock (made with the langoustines heads, a carrot, onion, celery branch, spices)
300g Carnaroli rice (plain or with tartufo or wild mushrooms)
1 shallot chopped
70 g butter, 1 tbsp good olive oil
100ml white wine or Noilly (dry vermouth)
5 tbsp grated Parmesan
some greens (broccoli, asparagus) blanched
juice and zest of one lemon
1 tsp grated ginger
2 tbsp single malt
salt, ground black pepper

Marinate the scallops with the lemon juice and zest and grated ginger. Place the mussels into a covered a pan and cook over medium heat until all mussels have opened. Drain them adding the cooking juices to the shellfish stock. Remove the mussels from their shells and set aside, keeping a few in their shell for decoration. Warm the stock in a pan.

In another pan, melt the butter with oil and add the chopped shallot. Cook it slowly until the shallot is soft. Add the rice, stir for one minute or two. Add the wine, lower the heat.
Add 2 ladles of stock. Stir continuously. When the rice has absorbed the liquid, add another ladle and carry on slowly, ladle by ladle, continuing stirring. Season.

The rice starts becoming creamy. Add the blanched vegetables. Carry on stirring. When the rice is creamy but a little al dente, add 3/4 of the Parmesan. Stir. Keep warm over a low heat.
In a pan, melt the butter, sauté langoustines and scallops, just for one minute on each side. Add the mussels. Take the shellfish out of the pan. Deglaze the pan with the single malt and add this to the risotto.

Divide the risotto between 6 warm plates. Add a knob of butter. Sprinkle with Parmesan. Serve the risotto topped with the langoustines, scallops and mussels, arrange the mussels in their shells among the other shellfish.

WHISKIES TO MATCH

PROFILE
This very flavoursome dish needs to be paired with a complex whisky, marked by vanilla sweetness, hence matured in a first fill bourbon cask. A medium peated whisky will be perfect.

SUGGESTIONS
Cù Bocan Virgin Oak
Ardbeg Perpetuum
Bruichladdich - Islay Barley 2006
Auchentoshan Virgin Oak second release
Port Askaig 12 Year Old (The Whisky Exchange)

Monkfish wrapped in pancetta, with fennel sauce laced with whisky

Monkfish has a firm flesh that allows it to be cooked as a roast. Pancetta adds a meaty touch which changes the approach to fish.

For the fish

1,2 kg monkfish (skinned and cut into 6 pieces)
12 rashers of pancetta
2 tbsp olive oil
2 tbsp grain mustard
3 tbsp chopped parsley
2 fennel leaves
sprig of thyme
ground black pepper, pinch of chili
1 shallot (finely chopped)

For the sauce

1 fennel bulb
2 tbsp double cream
juice of half a lemon
salt, ground black pepper
2 tbsp whisky

Preheat the oven (210°C - Gas mark 6/7). Chop the shallot and two fennel leaves. Place in a greased oven dish with the thyme. Open each piece of monkfish down the middle. Mix the spices, the olive oil, the mustard and the parsley. Spread a tablespoon of the mixture on the monkfish. Close and wrap each piece with two rashers of pancetta. Place in the dish and cook for 15 minutes.

Meanwhile, cut the fennel bulb into 4 pieces and cook it for 10 minutes in salted boiling water. Blend the fennel with a little cooking water. Add the cream and the lemon juice. Reduce over high heat until a velouté sauce texture is achieved. Then add the whisky, season and keep warm.

Place a piece of monkfish on each plate, spoon the fennel coulis around. Serve with boiled potatoes or rice.

WHISKIES TO MATCH

PROFILE

The aniseed flavour of the dish speaks out for a bourbon cask matured whisky. The pancetta adds a meaty touch that goes with an oaky note. So a double matured malt features well.

SUGGESTIONS

Glenmorangie Lasanta 12 Year Old
Asyla (Compass Box)
Glen Moray 12 Year old
Bushmills 10 Year Old
Oban Distillers Edition

Apricot and almond lamb tagine

Moroccan tagine is a magic dish. it will take you to a wonderful world of fragrant spices and bright colours. Lamb is my favorite meat for tagines and the dried fruit and nuts make a perfect match with whisky.

A selection of spices:
2 tsp ground coriander, 2 tsp cumin, 1 1/2 tsp ground ginger, 1 tsp chilli powder, 1 tsp cinnamon, 1 tsp ground cardamom, 1/2 tsp allspice
2 tsp salt, ground black pepper
a few threads of saffron
3 tbsp olive oil
the grated zest and juice of 1 lemon and 1 orange
1tbsp clear honey
1.2kg diced lamb (shoulder)
100ml chicken stock
100g dried apricots (chopped)
150ml Earl Grey tea
3 tbsp whisky
60g blanched almonds
1 chopped medium onion

Combine the spices and salt in a large bowl. Add the oil, the honey, the lemon, the orange zest and half the juice and stir to form a paste. Add the lamb and the chopped onion and stir until well coated in paste. Cover and marinate for 3 hours in the fridge.
Soak the apricots in the Earl Grey tea for one hour. Drain and then macerate in the whisky for 30 minutes.

Preheat the oven (180°C Gas mark 6).

In a frying pan, sauté the lamb in olive oil until golden. Then place the lamb mixture (with any of the marinate left in the bowl) into a tagine dish or a casserole with a lid. Add the stock and remaining citrus fruit juice. Stir until well combined.
Cover and cook for 1 hour. Then stir in the dried apricot and almonds. Cook, covered for a further 50 min.

Serve with couscous sprinkled with toasted pine kernel and cinnamon.

WHISKIES TO MATCH

PROFILE

The tagine is spicy but not hot, the addition of honey and apricots brings it a sweet touch too. Select a fruity whisky with a hint of sherry (dried fruit aromas) and a long finish. Intensity is the key.

SUGGESTIONS

Glenmorangie 18 Year Old
The BenRiach 16 Year old
Glengoyne 21 Year Old
Glenfiddich 18 Year Old
Springbank 18 Year Old

Venison fillet marinated in whisky
with chestnuts, wild mushrooms and root vegetables

This rich autumnal meaty dish retains the fragrances of a walk in the forest. I personally find it difficult to eat venison because I love seeing deer roaming on the slopes of the hills on Jura or Islay. But venison is a favorite for many. So ...

600g venison fillet (cut into 6 steaks)

For the marinade
3 tbsp of cocoa 'grué'
(the chopped toasted bean)
1tbsp juniper berries,
1tbsp black peppercorns
60ml olive oil
a pinch of sugar
2 tbsp single malt

For the sauce
500ml veal (or beef) stock
250ml red wine (or port)
1 tbsp single malt

For the vegetables
18 cooked chestnuts
100g dried mushrooms
4 shallots (chopped)
40g butter
60g duck fat
400g root vegetables
(parsnips, carrots, celeriac)
salt, ground black pepper

The day before the preparation, marinate the venison with all the ingredients of the marinade.

Prepare the vegetables. Rehydrate mushrooms by soaking them 20 minutes in warm water in a bowl. Wash them several times and drain. Cook them 2 minutes in a frying pan with the shallots and half the butter. Season. Keep aside.

Pre-heat the oven (200°C - Gas mark 6). Peel the root vegetables and cut them into 'chips'. In a pan, brown them in the duck fat for a few minutes then place them in a greased oven dish and cook for 25 minutes until they are cooked but still a little crisp.

Prepare the sauce. In a saucepan, boil the stock with the drained juice of the marinade and the wine until 2/3 reduced. Heat the chestnuts in the sauce. Keep warm over low heat.

In a hot pan, seal the venison fillets in a little duck fat. Take them out of the pan and keep them in a warm dish. Deglaze the pan with the sauce, adding a dash of single malt at the end. Finish cooking the meat in the oven for a few minutes (depending on how you like it cooked). On warm plates, place the mushrooms in the middle, then the venison steaks on the top and lace with sauce. Add the root vegetables on the side.

─ WHISKIES TO MATCH ─

PROFILE

We are talking intense flavours here. So a single malt matured in a sherry cask (first fill preferably) will feature brilliantly.

SUGGESTIONS

Aberlour a'bunadh
Benrinnes 15 Year Old - Flora & Fauna
The Macallan Ruby
The Dalmore King Alexander III
Mortlach 15 Year Old
(Gordon & MacPhail)

Filet mignon of pork rolled in grain mustard and nuts, black pudding flan with an apple sauce

Apples and pork make a delicious combination. Black pudding brings in a rustic touch which finds the perfect match with the malty notes of the whisky. Easy to prepare, not expensive and more re-fined than it may appear.

For the pork
1,3 kg pork filet mignon (usually 2 fillets)
1 tbsp olive oil
30g butter
6 shallots (in thin slices)
1 tbsp heather honey
3 tbsp grain mustard
a mix of ground spices : pepper, ginger, nutmeg, pinch of cinnamon
3 tbsp crushed hazelnuts
thyme and bay leaf
2 tbsp sherry vinegar
1 tbsp double cream
1 cooked apple (pureed)
3 tbsp whisky

For the black pudding flans
2 slices of Stornoway black pudding (cut into dice)
2 eggs (beaten)
4 oatcakes (crumbled)
2 apples grated
2 tbsp whisky

Preheat the oven at 170°C (Gas mark 3) for slow cooking.

Mix the mustard with the spices and the nuts, add a dash of whisky and spread the mixture on the filet mignon. Place in a greased baking tray with the water and the juices, the thyme and bay leaf.

Slow cook for 90 minutes. Baste it lightly (to avoid losing the spicy crust) but regularly.

Meanwhile, prepare the black pudding flan, mix all the ingredients in a bowl. Pour into greased ramequins (or a bigger dish and cut into squares). Cook in the oven for 25 minutes. When the pork is cooked, let it rest 10 minutes before slicing. Strain the cooking juice and heat it on the hob. Add the vinegar and boil at high heat to reduce by half. Add the apple purée and the cream. Whisk to obtain a smooth sauce. Off the heat, add the whisky.

Heat the butter and olive oil in a pan. Add the shallots. Brush the filet mignon with honey. Seal it in the pan on all sides. Take the shallots and the meat out of the pan. Discard the excess fat and pour in 200ml of water. Stir to collect all the juices left from the meat.

Slice the pork into medallions, place a black pudding flan on each plate, a few pork medal-lions on the side and spoon the sauce around them.

Serve with roast vegetables.

WHISKIES TO MATCH

PROFILE
The apple purée in the sauce will be the bridge. The best choice will be a fruity whisky with a good malty base. Preferably unpeated. Or very lightly.

SUGGESTIONS
Glen Garioch 12 Year Old
Knockando 12 Year Old
Benromach 10 Year Old - 100% proof
Longmorn 16 Year Old
Jameson 18 Year Old

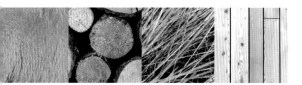

Haddock marinated in whisky with a lemon and butter sauce and tatties

The best haddock is known as 'Finnan Haddie'. The name derives from Findon, a small fishing village on the east coast of Scotland, south of Aberdeen. Haddock is traditionally smoked over wood shavings coming from whisky casks.

800g skinned Finnan (smoked) haddock
500ml milk
100ml natural yogourt
60ml whisky + 1 tbsp
ground black pepper
100g butter
juice of 1 lemon
2 tbsp chopped parsley
1kg potatoes (peeled and boiled)

Prepare the haddock marinade 48 hours ahead. Place the haddock fillets in a plastic container with a lid. In a bowl, mix carefully 200ml of milk, 200ml of water, the yogourt and 60ml of whisky. Pour this marinade over the haddock and place in the fridge for 2 days. Stir at least twice a day to make sure the haddock flesh is well impregnated by the marinade.

After two days, remove the haddock from the marinade, dry it on kitchen paper and discard the marinade. Put the haddock fillets in a large thick-based pan, add 250ml of water and 300ml of milk, enough to cover the fish. Do not add salt, haddock is naturally salted but use ground black pepper. Bring to a boil, then reduce the heat to simmering. Allow to cook for 12 to 15 minutes, according to the thickness of the haddock fillets. It is cooked when the flakes come off easily.

Melt the butter with the lemon juice. Add the ground black pepper and the last tablespoon of whisky. Divide the haddock fillets into 6 servings and place in a warm dish. Top with the sauce. Sprinkle with chopped parsley.
Serve with boiled potatoes ('pommes de terre à l'anglaise' in French).

WHISKIES TO MATCH

PROFILE
Avoid peated whiskies. Go for a malty whisky with a rich cereal character (bread, dry hay, meadow flowers, etc). A citrussy note will find a good bridge with the butter and lemon.

SUGGESTIONS
Glenkinchie 12 Year Old
Old Pulteney 12 Year Old
Cardhu 12 Year Old
Great King Street - Artist's Blend
(Compass Box)
Knockando 12 Year Old

Wild mushroom and butternut squash risotto

Vegetable marrows and mushrooms can't go wrong with whisky. The sweetness of the former and the earthy character of the latter perform a delightful 'pas de deux' in this autumnal dance.

400g butternut squash (peeled and cut in small dice)
2 tbsp single malt
1,5ltr chicken or vegetable stock
30g dried porcini mushrooms
240g wild mushrooms finely sliced
1 large pinch of ground coriander
1 big shallot finely chopped
270g Carnaroli rice
150ml white wine (or vermouth)
60g butter
100g grated Parmesan
1 tbsp chopped coriander
salt and ground black pepper

Rehydrate the porcini mushrooms by soaking them 20 minutes in warm water in a bowl. Wash them several times and drain. Gently heat the chicken stock in a pan. Add the mushrooms and warm in the stock. Remove them after 5 minutes and chop them. Reserve for later.

Preheat the oven (200°C - Gas mark 6). Place the butternut squash dice in an ovenproof dish, sprinkle with olive oil. Season with salt and black pepper. Roast in the oven for 25 minutes. then spray with the single malt. Keep warm.

Quickly wash the wild mushrooms and drain them. Melt 30g butter in a pan. Add the wild mushrooms and the coriander. Cook for 5 to 7 minutes. Reserve the mushrooms aside and pour the cooking juice into the chicken stock.
In the same pan, cook the shallot in the rest of the butter with a little olive oil without colouring it. Add the Carnaroli rice, stir and cook for 5 minutes then add the vermouth, keep stirring. Season with salt and pepper. When the rice has absorbed the liquid, pour in one ladle of stock. Continue to add stock in this way until the rice is tender but still with a slight bite. 5 Minutes before the end of cooking, add all the mushrooms. Add the Parmesan off the heat.
Divide between 6 plates. Top with the roasted butternut squash and fresh chopped coriander.

WHISKIES TO MATCH

PROFILE
The earthiness of the mushrooms will go well with a sherried malt but the sherry notes must not be overwhelming. Astringency and oakiness would spoil the broth! Go for second fill sherry casks.

SUGGESTIONS
Isle of Jura 16 Year Old
Highland Park 12 Year Old
Springbank 12 Year Old
Linkwood 15 Year Old (Gordon & MacPhail)
The Balvenie Double wood 12 Year Old

Roast guinea-fowl
with a malted stuffing and glazed quinces

This festive recipe will be a hit at your Christmas table. An elegant alternative to turkey or goose. Quinces bring in the sunny sweetness which we miss in winter.

1 guinea-fowl (just over 1,400kg) with its giblets
50g butter
2 shallots
4 long peppercorns, crushed
5 cubèbe peppercorns, crushed
2 tablespoons sherry (or malt) vinegar
1 thick slice gingerbread
salt and ground black pepper
6 slices of toast for service
For the stuffing
the guinea-fowl giblets
2 chopped shallots, 8 chopped dates
50g cottage cheese
50ml single malt
mixed spices : ground ginger, coriander seeds, white pepper corns
1 tbsp chopped parsley
3 oatcakes, crushed
1tbsp crushed pistacchios or hazelnuts (preferably toasted)
salt and ground black pepper
For the garnish
2 quinces
juice of half a lemon
3 tbsp demerara sugar
1 tbsp heather honey
ground black pepper
1 pinch of allspice

Prepare the stuffing. Chop the giblets (heart, liver and gizzard). Mix them in a bowl with all the ingredients of the stuffing

Pre-heat the oven (180°C - Gas mark 4). Carefully spoon the stuffing inside the guinea fowl and truss it. Brush the surface of the guinea-fowl with single malt and smear it with butter. Put it in a roasting tray. Add 200ml of water, the peppercorns, the sliced shallots and vinegar. Place the guinea-fowl in the oven for 75 minutes, baste it every 15 minutes. Season with salt only when cooked.

In the meantime, prepare the glazed quinces. Wash the quinces, cut them into 4 segments and core them. Bring to the boil 500 ml of water with the lemon, the demerara sugar, the honey and spices. Simmer the quince segments in this syrupy water until they are soft and glazed. Then peel them and place them in a dish. Add the skins of the quinces and reduce the syrup with the vinegar on a high heat by 2/3. Strain it and leave to cool.
Allow the roasted guinea-fowl to rest on a warm dish for 10 minutes. Strain the cooking juices through a fine sieve. Blend the gingerbread into crumbs and add to the sauce with the reduced quince syrup. Warm up the sauce.
Warm the quinces. Carve the guinea-fowl. Serve it with its stuffing on toast and the glazed quinces. Top the guinea-fowl with some sauce and serve the rest in a gravy-boat.

PROFILE

A celebration dish requires a celebration whisky. Complex, multilayered, offering an elegant oaky and spicy frame Hence an older whisky. A Laird of Speyside!

SUGGESTIONS

Glenfarclas 17 Year Old
Glenfiddich 19 Year Old - Age of Discovery
The Glenrothes 1978
Glen Grant Five Decades
The Glenlivet 21 Year Old

Breast of duck in a marmalade and whisky sauce with quinoa and dried fruit

Duck and orange make a tasty combination perfectly illustrated by the famous 'canard à l'orange'. The duck breast version is easier, quicker and just as delicious.

3 duck breasts (350g each)
1 tbsp sunflower oil
3 tbsp thincut marmalade
3 chopped shallots
30g butter
1 finely diced carrot
1 finely diced stick of celery
the juice of 2 oranges and zest of one
300ml tasty duck stock
1 large pinch of allspice
3 tbsp single malt
salt, ground black pepper
For the garnish
400g quinoa (or pearl barley)
120g dried fruit (sultanas, chopped apricot, crushed almonds or pistaccios)
2 tbsp single malt
60g butter
salt, ground black pepper

Marinate the dried fruit in 2 tablespoons of single malt with half the orange zest. In a pan, cook the quinoa (or pearl barley) in boiling salted water for 35 to 40 minutes. Strain, put in a large bowl, add butter (60g) and the marinated dried fruit. Season with salt and ground black pepper. Allow ro rest.

Melt the butter (30g) in a pan, add the shallots, the diced carrot and diced celery. Leave the vegetables to sweat until slightly coloured then add the stock and reduce by half. Pour the orange juice and the rest of the zest, add the marmalade and allspice. Simmer for 10 minutes. Season to taste. Strain and allow to cool.

Preheat the oven (180°C - Gas mark 4). Heat the oil in a frying pan, gently fry the duck breasts in the pan for 5 minutes, turning them once. Place the duck breasts in a dish (skin side uppermost) and bake in the oven for 15 minutes. Turn off the oven and allow to rest for 10 minutes.
Meanwhile, bring the orange sauce to the boil, reduce by one third until you obtain a syrupy sauce. Add the single malt at the end and stir.
Reheat the dried fruit quinoa in a pan over a low heat. Divide between the plates. Slice the duck breasts into thin slices. Place them on the plate besides the quinoa. Top with sauce.

PROFILE

Two types of whiskies will pair with this tasty dish. A single malt with a sherry influence or a peated malt.

SUGGESTIONS

Lagavulin 16 Year Old
The Macallan Fine Oak 18 Year Old
Glen Grant 170th Anniversary
Benromach 15 Year Old
Bowmore 18 Year Old

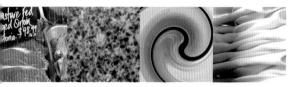

Filet of Beef with Périgourdine Sauce

Here is another festive dish. The sauce Périgourdine is a classic of French Haute Cuisine, slightly simplified here but just as tasty.

1,2 kg fillet beef, cut into 6 steaks
1 tbsp sunflower oil
30g butter
For the Périgourdine sauce
1 medium onion
500ml beef stock
1 bouquet garni
50g foie gras (cut in small dice)
1 small tin of truffle extract
2 tbsp single malt
salt, ground black pepper

Prepare the sauce. Melt the butter in a pan, add the chopped onion, fry until golden, add the beef stock into the pan. Season with salt and ground black pepper, add the bouquet garni. Simmer for 20 minutes. Then reduce by half on high heat. Strain the sauce. Whilst still warm add the diced foie gras and whisk until melted. Finish with the single malt and truffle extract. Reheat and keep warm on a very low heat.

Warm the oil and butter in a pan. Cook the beef steaks 3 to 6 minutes, depending on preference (from rare to well-cooked). Place the steaks on warm plates. Spoon the Périgourdine sauce on top of the steaks. Serve with French beans and a gratin dauphinois.

FLAVOUR TIP
The whole beef filet can also be cooked in puff pastry. It will remain tender and juicy.

WHISKIES TO MATCH

PROFILE
A sherry cask matured single malt will suit that rich dish.

SUGGESTIONS
Dailuaine 16 Year Old - Flora & Fauna
The GlenDronach 15 Year Old - revival
The Glenlivet Nadùrra Oloroso
Glenrothes Sherry Reserve
Aberfeldy 21 Year Old

CHEESE AND DESSERTS

The cheese platter

This can be the hub of a friendly improvised meal. Add a salad, some fruit and ... a few good drams. Everyone will be happy.

The choice of cheeses

Pairing a whisky (whatever the style and provenance) with a cheese platter is one of the trickiest challenges as cheeses offer such a variety of flavours and textures. To achieve a harmonious match, it is important to follow a few principles.

Offer a choice of whiskies and not only one if you mix different styles of cheeses.

If you can only serve one whisky, don't mix mature cheeses and fresh cheeses, such as a Comté matured for 36 months and a fresh goat cheese. They are miles apart.

Always find a 'bridge' which will link the food and the liquid: nuts, grapes, apples or a chutney, even honey in some cases.

Blue cheeses should not be presented with creamy cheeses such as Brie or Camembert. It can be very interesting to offer a variety of blue cheeses from the mildest to the sharpest, from the creamiest to the driest. They strike a good balance with pears, pine nuts and celery.

Biscuits and oatcakes traditionally accompany cheese in Britain. The French would prefer bread. Why not be adventurous and try different types of bread, plain, with raisins, nuts, figs, sourdough bread, toasted or not, alongside oatcakes?

Here is an example of an ideal platter: the varied selection of cheeses will be paired with, at least, a choice of two whiskies.

WHISKIES TO MATCH

PROFILE

It all depends on the cheese chosen. The Blue cheese will pair best with a peated whisky. Creamy or not very mature cheese will require a young single malt or single grain, mostly matured in ex-bourbon casks but with a nutty and malty profile. Mature cheeses such as Cheddar or Comté go wonderfully with an old fruity whisky (with a sherry influence).

SUGGESTIONS

(for the cheese platter photographed)
Hedonism (Compass Box)
The Glenlivet Founder's Reserve
Aberlour 18 Year Old
Glengoyne 10 Year Old
Lagavulin 16 Year Old

Fresh cheese, mango and honey waffle

This light combination of fluffy cheese, fruit, honey and whisky on a freshly baked waffle makes an unusual dessert. You can also present the cheese as an ice cream by putting it in an ice cream maker for 15 minutes before serving. Ideal for a brunch!

For the cheese
300g fresh cheese (either a soft goat cheese or a cream cheese)
2 tbsp whisky
1 mango
1 tsp honey
1 tsp grated lime zest
juice of half a lime
pinch of black pepper
For the waffles
180g plain flour
30g caster sugar
1 tbsp liquid honey
2/3 tsp baking powder
2 eggs (yolks and white separated)
350 ml semi-skimmed milk
60g melted butter
To finish
1 tbsp whisky, 1 tbsp clear honey

Peel the mango and dice it into small cubes. Marinate the diced pulp in the whisky with the honey, the lime zest, the lime juice and black pepper for 10 minutes. Put the cheese in a bowl and fold in the marinated mango and the syrup. Turn the waffle maker on.

To make the waffle, mix the dry ingredients in a bowl. In a separate bowl, mix the milk, the egg yolks and the melted butter. Add the milk mixture to the dry ingredients and stir until you get a smooth batter. Whisk the egg whites until stiff peaks are formed and gently fold into the waffle batter. When the waffle maker is hot, pour one ladle of the batter onto each plate and cook for 4 to 5 minutes until golden. Keep the waffles warm in the oven.

To serve, place a warm waffle on each plate, put one scoop of mango cheese on each one. Cover with a little honey and a drizzle of whisky. Serve immediately.

WHISKIES TO MATCH

PROFILE
Go for a whisky 'pâtissier' (with dessert-like notes), buttery, fruity with an almondy aftertaste. Irish whiskeys have an exotic fruit nose and palate, which will perfectly fit the mango cheese.

SUGGESTIONS
Glenmorangie Nectar d'or
Mackmyra Midnattssol
Amrut
Green Spot
Redbreast 12 Year Old

Fruit and nut Cheddar slice

Enjoy a whole Cheddar cheese layered with dried fruit harmoniously marinated in whisky. Once again, it could replace the sweet.

300g medium mature cheddar
A mix of dried fruit: apricots, dates, raisins, cranberries, all chopped (80g)
A mix of nuts: pecan nuts, hazelnuts, walnuts, chopped (60g)
3 tbsp single malt
black pepper
a pinch of ground cinnamon

To be prepared a week before serving.
Marinate the fruit, the nuts and the spices in the whisky and allow to soak for 48h.

Cut the block of cheese into three slices (horizontally). Spread a layer of the fruit and nut stuffing onto one slice. Place the next slice of cheese on top. And repeat the layering. Wrap tightly in cling film. Leave in a cool place to set (preferably not in the fridge as this may be too cold).

To serve, carefully unwrap the cheese. Slice carefully making sure you keep the fruit filling in place. Serve with toasted bread or oatcakes and a light salad.

WHISKIES TO MATCH

PROFILE
A complex malty and fruity single malt with a touch of sherry, but not too oaky.

SUGGESTIONS
Aberlour 16 Year Old
Mortlach 15 Year Old (Gordon & MacPhail)
Tomatin 18 Year Old
Old Pulteney 17 Year Old
Dalwhinnie Distillers Edition

Comté and mushroom parcel

An ideal first course, the smooth Comté and mushrooms filling complements the crisp, just baked filo pastry.

400g button mushrooms
1 pinch ground coriander
60g butter
6 filo pastry sheets
6 slices of mature Comté
salt, ground black pepper
a large pinch of fleur de sel
1 tbsp whisky

Wash and chop the mushrooms. Melt 40g butter in a pan, gently sauté the mushrooms with the coriander over medium heat. Season with salt and pepper. Drain the mushrooms reserving the cooking juices. Reduce the cooking juices to the equivalent of one tablespoon of liquid in the hot pan. Pour over the mushrooms.

Melt the remaining butter and use to brush the filo pastry sheets. Lay the filo sheet with the long edge towards you. Place a Comté slice on the first third, from the left. Add a tablespoon of cooked mushrooms. Fold the filo pastry working from left to right, to make a parcel. Brush the surface with the melted butter. Sprinkle with fleur de sel.

Bake 5 to 8 minutes in a hot oven (220°C - Gas mark 7). Immediately spray whisky over each parcel and serve on a bed of salad.

FLAVOUR TIP
The tasty bonus: add a teaspoon of truffle oil when cooking the mushrooms.

WHISKIES TO MATCH

PROFILE
A sherried whisky with an earthy touch, or a bourbon with a good proportion of rye. A spicy whisky can also complement this fruity cheese.

SUGGESTIONS
Aberlour 18 Year Old
Basil Hayden's Small Batch
The Spice Tree (Compass Box)
Glenmorangie Companta
Glengoyne 18 Year Old

Pear and Stilton tart

This delicious cheese tart can end a meal, be used as a starter or as a main course for a light lunch, served with a green salad. The tang of the blue cheese is toned down by the flavour of the pear.

For the pastry
200g plain flour
100g soft butter
1 pinch of salt
1 pinch of ground cinnamon
1 small egg (beaten)
For the filling
150g Stilton
3 tbsp whisky
3 pears (Conference)
juice of half a lemon
2 tbsp pine nuts
To finish
20g melted butter
1 tbsp whisky

Prepare the shortcrust pastry. In a bowl, sieve the flour, add salt, cinnamon and butter. Rub the butter into the flour with your fingertips until you get fine breadcrumbs. Add the beaten egg and knead gently into a ball. Wrap the dough in cling film and leave it to rest in the fridge for 30 minutes.

Preheat the oven (200°C - Gas mark 6). Roll out the pastry and line six greased individual tart dishes. Place in the fridge for 30 minutes to chill. Then bake 'blind' for 20 minutes (Line the pastry tarts with greaseproof paper and fill with dry beans to prevent the pastry from swelling).

Meanwhile, cut the Stilton into thin slices and marinate in the whisky for 20 minutes. Peel and core the pears and cut them into thin slices with lemon juice to avoid the pears turning black.

Remove the paper and beans from the tart cases. Let the tart cases cool for a few minutes. Line the bottom of each one with the Stilton and pear slices. Brush the surface with a mixture of whisky and melted butter. Sprinkle with pine nuts. Place under the grill for 6 to 8 minutes.

WHISKIES TO MATCH

PROFILE
Peated whiskies will be the best choice. The alternative can be a single malt with a Port wood finish. Or a combination of both.

SUGGESTIONS
The Peat Monster (Compass Box)
Kilchoman Port Cask matured
Ardmore Legacy
BenRiach Curiositas
CI6 - Elements of Islay - The Whisky Exchange

Marshmallow icecream and red fruit salad laced with whisky

The light tanginess of the yogurt enhances the red fruit flavours. Subtle and eye-catching, this sweet will delight your guests by its freshness and simplicity.

For the icecream
200g marshmallows (white and pink)
3 tbsp double cream
500g Greek yogurt
juice of half a lemon
For the fruit salad
600g mixed red fruit (strawberries, raspberries, blackcurrants, redcurrants)
2 tbsp cherry or strawberry jam
juice of half a lemon
3 tbsp single malt
pinch of black pepper
sprigs of mint (chopped)

Place the fruit in a large bowl. Set aside 6 small strawberries for decoration. Melt the jam with the lemon juice a few seconds in a microwave or a saucepan on the hob. Add to the fruit with whisky and black pepper. Stir gently. Put in the fridge.

Make the icecream. Melt the marshmallows with the cream in a bowl placed over a pan of simmering water (bain-marie). Stir until the marshmallows are completely melted in the cream. Remove from the bain-marie and allow to cool. In a bowl, whisk the yogurt with the lemon juice. Add to the marshmallow mixture and place in the icecream maker or in a suitable container in the freezer (if using this method, remove from the freezer after one hour and whisk to break up any ice crystals).

Divide the fruit salad into 6 glasses. Sprinkle with chopped mint. Top with a scoop of icecream and decorate with a strawberry.

A QUICK VERSION

If you don't have time to make an icecream with the marshmallows, just cut a dozen in small dice and add to the salad.

THE FLAVOUR TIP

A pinch of pepper added to the fruit acts as a flavour enhancer. There is no need to add sugar. The natural fruit sweetness is enough.

WHISKIES TO MATCH

PROFILE
A floral and fruity whisky will find harmony with the fruit and the smooth texture of the icecream. A Port wood finish (on a young whisky) makes a good match with red fruit.

SUGGESTIONS
Cragganmore Distillers Edition
Glenmorangie Quinta Ruban 12 Year Old
Edradour 2003 - Port Cask Matured
Aultmore 12 Year Old
Tyrconnell Port Finish

Rhubarb crumble

A classic, revisited with the addition of crystallised ginger. I love making this sweet as I have beautiful rhubarb in my garden. The crumble has a Scottish touch as oatmeal is used. It gives a coarse crumble, crunchy and tasty.

700g rhubarb stalks
80g caster sugar
60g crystallised ginger (chopped)
130g plain flour
70g oatmeal
3 tbsp chopped hazelnuts
90g demerara sugar
130g unsalted butter
1 good pinch of fleur de sel

Clean and wash the rhubarb stalks. Cut them in 3 cm long sections. Place them in a baking dish. Sprinkle with caster sugar and crystallised ginger. Cook for 15 minutes in the oven (200°C, Gas mark 6).

In a bowl, rub together the butter, the flour, the oatmeal, the hazelnuts, the fleur de sel and demerara sugar until you obtain rough crumbs (hence the name of the sweet!). Remove the rhubarb from the oven and cover with the crumble mixture. Place back into the oven for a further 20/25 minutes, until the crumble is golden brown.

Serve cold or warm.

THE FLAVOUR TIP
You can serve with vanilla icecream or a vanilla custard or crème fraîche. In Summer, fresh strawberries make a refreshing side dish.

WHISKIES TO MATCH

PROFILE
A fruity whisky (single malt or blend) with a good malty core will find a good match with the cereals and the nuts. The slight tangy flavour of the rhubarb will balance the malty sweetness.

SUGGESTIONS
The Balvenie Signature
Craigellachie 13 Year Old
Jameson 18 Year Old
Miyagikyo 12 Year Old
Four Roses

Cranachan

Cranachan is a traditional Scottish recipe which used ingredients that were available on the farm such as home grown raspberries, local honey and 'crowdie', a soft cheese found in Scotland. You can also make it with a soft curd cheese. It gives an interesting sour touch.

100g pinhead oatmeal
300ml whipping cream
(or curd cheese)
250g raspberries
2 tbsp heather honey
3 tbsp single malt

Toast the oatmeal lightly in a dry pan on the hob. Put aside to cool.

Whisk the cream until thick enough to leave a ribbon trail. Add the honey, the whisky and 3/4 of toasted oatmeal. Fold the mixture together.

Set aside some raspberries for garnishing. Take 6 glasses. Alternate layers of raspberries and of the oatmeal mixture. Allow to set in the fridge. Before serving, garnish with raspberries and a ribbon of honey. Sprinkle the rest of the toasted oatmeal.

Serve with shortbread.

THE SMART TIP

'Revisit' the Cranachan by making it into an icecream. Roll the icecream ball in pinhead oatmeal before serving. Serve with raspberries and a raspberry coulis.

WHISKIES TO MATCH

PROFILE

A bourbon matured whisky, fruity with a floral touch, will go along with the delicate flavour of raspberries. Speyside malts match especially well with honeyed dishes.

SUGGESTIONS

BenRiach Heart of Speyside
Glencadam 10 Year Old
Glann ar Mor
The Glenlivet Founder Reserve
Glenmorangie Original 10 Year Old

Whisky flavoured strawberry and lemon Charlotte

You will impress your guests with this colourful sweet, as delightful for the eye as for the tastebuds. It takes time to prepare but you can easily make the biscuit base and the lemon curd the day before.

For the shortbread base
70g ground hazelnuts
30g chopped hazelnuts
1 egg
1 pinch of salt
2 tbsp caster sugar
150g plain flour
120g unsalted butter
For the lemon curd and strawberries
3 lemons (juice and grated zest)
180g caster sugar
85g unsalted butter
2 gelatine leaves
3 eggs
3 tbsp whisky
300g large strawberries
For the coulis
200g strawberries
juice from half a lemon
2 tbsp whisky
ground black pepper
a few drops balsamic vinegar

Prepare the shorbread base. Beat the egg in a bowl. In a separate bowl, mix together the dry ingredients. Cut the butter into pieces and rub it into the dry ingredients. Add the beaten egg and knead together to form a soft but not sticky dough. Set aside in the fridge for 30 minutes.

Prepare the lemon curd. Let the leaves of gelatine soak for 10 minutes in cold water then squeeze them tightly. Cut the butter into small pieces and put it into a bowl placed over a pan of simmering water (bain-marie). Add the sugar, the lemon juice and grated zest and stir until the sugar and butter are melted. Add the gelatine leaves and stir until melted.

Whisk the eggs in a bowl and pour into the lemon juice mixture while keeping on whisking. Stir until the preparation thickens (8 to 10 minutes). Remove from the bain-marie and allow to cool for a few minutes then stir in the whisky.

Preheat the oven (200°C - Gas mark 6). Roll out the dough out about 5 mm thick. Use individual stainless ring moulds (4cm high x 6cm wide) to cut 6 rounds in the shortbread. Place each round within a ring mould on a greased baking sheet and cook in the oven for 15 minutes. Then place the pastry rounds and their moulds onto individual plates. Leave to cool.

Rinse the strawberries, hull them and cut them into two halves. Line the inside of the moulds with the strawberries, putting the flat side of the strawberry against the mould. Fill in with the lemon and whisky curd up to 2/3 of the height of the strawberries. Keep the Charlottes in the fridge for 4 hours at least.

Prepare the coulis. Keep six smaller strawberries to garnish the top of the curd. Blend the rest of the fruit with the lemon juice, pepper and whisky. Put through a sieve to give a smooth coulis. Remove the Charlotte from the mould. Drizzle strawberry coulis round the Charlotte and a few drops of balsamic vinegar.

PROFILE

A light citrussy single malt or grain whisky, matured in bourbon cask will bring out the tangy character of this Charlotte. The buttery base balances the tartness of the lemon.

SUGGESTIONS

Glen Moray Classic
Aultmore 12 Year Old
Bowmore Small Batch
Vive le Zeste! - 1998/2014
  (Wemyss Whiskies)
Kilbeggan 8 Year Old (single grain)

Nougat glacé and caramelized apricot

The secret of this sweet is to buy the best quality hazelnuts (from Piedmont in Italy) and pistachios (from Sicily). Try different fruit (and different whiskies) to vary the pleasures!

3 egg whites
80g caster sugar
3 tsp clear honey
50g hazelnuts, 50g pistachios,
50g almonds (flaked or whole)
A few whole hazelnuts for the decoration
50g dried apricots
50ml single malt
300ml whipping cream
1 tin of apricot halves
2tbsp demerara sugar

The day before, cut the dried apricots into four and soak them in the whisky.

Chop the different nuts, and toast them lightly in a pan on the hob. Then sprinkle 40g of sugar over the nuts while still on the hob. Stir gently until the sugar is caramelized and coats the nuts. Pour onto a sheet of greaseproof paper and leave to cool and then divide into small pieces. Do the same with the whole nuts ready for decoration.

In a pan, pour the honey and add the remaining sugar. Bring to the boil and continue to heat until you reach 120°C (about 4 minutes). Beat the egg whites to stiff peaks and slowly pour in the warm honey mixture. Continue beating until the meringue has cooled (this is what we call Italian meringue).

Whip the cream to stiff peaks and add to the Italian meringue. Then add the fruit (with the whisky) and the caramelized nuts. Stir gently. Place in a loaf tin (approximately 25 x 11 cm) and freeze for 12 hours.

Before serving, reserve 6 apricot halves, blend the rest with a little of the syrup to obtain a thick coulis. Sprinkle the demerara sugar on the halves and caramelize under the grill or with a blowtorch. Remove the nougat glacé from its tin, place a slice on each plate, a caramelized nut and an apricot half and finish with the coulis.

WHISKIES TO MATCH

PROFILE
Go for a reasonably matured fruity whisky, according to the nature of the fruit you will add. This dessert allows a large spectrum of matchings, depending on the nature of the coulis. Caramelized nuts make a flexible bridge with all fruity whiskies.

SUGGESTIONS
Glenrothes 1988
Longmorn 16 Year Old
Glen Keith 19 Year Old - 1995/2014
Glenmorangie Nectar d'Or 12 Year Old
Arran - the Amarone cask Finish

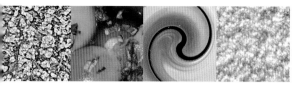

Vanilla Panna Cotta with salted caramel sauce, peaches poached in spices and nougatine

A Panna Cotta offers a delicious base for creativity. You can use a whole range of summer fruit, add crunchy ingredients, use a variety of containers. Be daring!

3 fresh peaches
pinch of ground ginger and cinnamon
1 tbsp quince jelly or honey
juice of half a lemon

For the panna cotta
500 ml double cream
1 vanilla pod (opened)
75g caster sugar
2 gelatine leaves
3 tbsp single malt

For the salted caramel sauce
100g caster sugar
150 ml single cream
50 g butter
Pinch of fleur de sel

For decoration
80g flaked almonds
2tbsp sugar

Make the panna cotta, Bring the cream to a simmer in a saucepan with the vanilla pod and sugar. Soak the gelatine leaves in cold water for 10 minutes. Drain and squeeze and add to the mixture. Add the whisky. Then pour into ramekins. Set in the fridge for 3 to 4 hours.

Make the caramel sauce. Put the sugar in a pan over a low heat and let it melt. When it is a deep golden colour, take it from the heat and add the cream slowly. Add the butter cut into small dice piece by piece and the fleur de sel and whisk. Keep in the pan and warm it again just before serving the panna cotta.

Peel the peaches and cut each into two halves, removing the stone. Make a syrup with 200 ml of water and the quince jelly, plus the spices. Bring it to the boil. Put in the half peaches. Cook for 5 minutes. Add the lemon juice. Then drain the peaches on kitchen roll. Put the almonds in a pan with the sugar over a medium heat. Allow the sugar to melt and caramelize the almonds. Remove from the heat and pour onto a sheet of greaseproof paper. Leave to cool.

To serve, turn the panna cotta onto a plate. Cut the peaches in slices and place on the side. Spoon the salted caramel sauce around. Decorate with caramelized almonds.

WHISKIES TO MATCH

PROFILE
A fruity (summer fruit aromatic profile) and creamy whisky will be perfect. The salted caramel sauce will also pair well with a medium peated whisky.

SUGGESTIONS
Glenfarclas 21 year Old
Springbank 10 Year Old
Caol Ila 1995 - 19 Year Old - Signatory Vintage
Bruichladdich (The Classic)
anCnoc Cutter

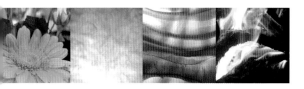

Mango Cappucino, topped with whisky coconut cream

The analogy with the Cappucino is more visual than aromatic of course. But this novel presentation will please even people who are not very keen on desserts.

3 perfectly ripe mangos
200g Greek yogurt
2 tbsp caster sugar
spices: 1/2 tsp ground ginger, 1/2 tsp ground coriander, a large pinch black pepper

For the coconut cream

250ml coconut milk
1tsp grated lime zest
1 tbsp caster sugar
3 tbsp whisky
1 pinch ground ginger

Peel the mangos, cut the flesh into large dice. Blend them with the yogurt, the caster sugar and spices. Divide the purée into 6 coffee cups or glasses. Do not fill them up, leave 2 cm at the top. Place in the freezer for 45 minutes.

Get the cups out of the freezer 10 minutes before serving.

Pour the coconut milk into a bowl, add the lime zest, sugar and whisky. Whisk vigorously to get a frothy mixture. Spoon onto the mango purée. Sprinkle with the ground ginger.

Serve immediately with a stem ginger shortbread.

WHISKIES TO MATCH

PROFILE
A fruity whisky - Irish whiskeys feature particularly well with their exotic aromatic character - with a silky or satin-like texture will mingle well with the creamy and frothy 'cappucino'.

SUGGESTIONS
Springbank 21 Year Old
Jameson Signature Reserve
Tyrconnell Madeira Finish
Amrut
Teeling Single Malt Irish Whiskey

Pears in a whisky flavoured quince jelly with ricotta mousse and crumbly ginger shortbread

Quince, one of the tastiest autumn fruit, features with pears in this recipe. A delicate and light sweet with a spicy twist.

1 small tin of pears in syrup
half a vanilla pod (opened)
1 tbsp lemon juice
3 gelatine leaves
4 tbsp quince jelly
a pinch of ground black pepper
300g ricotta
50g crème fraîche
2 tbsp muscovado sugar
3 tbsp single malt
3 ginger shortbread biscuits (crumbled)

Drain the pears but keep the syrup. Cut the pears into small dice. Soak the gelatine leaves in cold water for 10 minutes. Boil the pear syrup with the vanilla pod and the lemon juice. Take off the heat. Drain two gelatine leaves, squeeze and melt them in the warm syrup. Divide the pears into six glass bowls. Cover with the syrup and place in the fridge for a minimum of 30 minutes to allow to set.

Warm the quince jelly in the microwave or in a pan on the hob. Add a tablespoon of single malt and the last drained and squeezed gelatine leaf. Season with pepper. Keep aside.

Melt the muscovado sugar into the rest of the single malt. Whisk the ricotta and the cream together for a few minutes and add the sugar and whisky mixture.

Take the pears out of the fridge, pour 1 tablespoon of the quince jelly mixture over the pears in each bowl and then add the ricotta mousse. Keep in the fridge until service. Then sprinkle the crumbled shortbread biscuits on top.

WHISKIES TO MATCH

PROFILE
Choose a fresh and fruity malt like a light Speyside or a fragrant Highland malt. A fruity Irish whiskey, will bring out the pear flavours. A guaranteed success.

SUGGESTIONS
The Glenlivet 12 Year Old
Glenfiddich 12 Year Old
Balblair 1997
Scapa 16 Year Old
Tyrconnell

Gingerbread icecream with an orange salad

A spicy icecream, mingling perfectly with the citrussy notes of the fruit salad. The crunchy texture of the chocolate offers an elegant and harmonious array of flavours. If you add the perfect whisky... it is a marriage made in heaven!

For the orange salad
3 blood oranges
2 tbsp orange thin-cut marmalade
2 tbsp of whisky
1 pinch of black pepper
For the icecream
100ml semi-skimmed milk
200ml double cream
4 egg yolks
40g caster sugar
3 gingerbread slices (e.g Jamaïcan ginger cake)
2 tbsp chopped dark chocolate
(60% cocoa content minimum)

Blend the gingerbread until you get fine crumbs. Set aside.

Make the custard ('crème anglaise' in French). Bring the milk and the cream to the boil in a saucepan. Whisk the egg yolks with the sugar in a separate bowl. Pour the warm milk and the cream over the egg yolks. Stir the mixture, return to saucepan and put back on the heat. Cook at medium heat for 5 to 7 minutes. The cream must not boil, so continue to stir. When it starts to thicken, remove from the heat.

Let the custard cool for a little while then add the crumbled gingerbread. Stir until the gingerbread is well integrated. Place in the icecream maker or in a suitable container in the freezer (if using this method, remove from the freezer after one hour and whisk to break up any ice crystals).

Using a sharp knife, peel and segment the oranges into a bowl. Melt the marmalade in the microwave or a pan on the hob. Add to the fruit with the pepper and the whisky.

Divide into 6 bowls. Spoon the icecream on the top. Sprinkle with chopped chocolate.

WHISKIES TO MATCH

PROFILE
Orange and chocolate call for a whisky influenced by a sherry cask maturation or with a spicy oaky frame. But not too pronounced. Avoid peated whiskies for this combination.

SUGGESTIONS
Aultmore 21 Year Old
Balblair 2004 - 1st release Sherry matured
Blair Atholl 12 Year Old - Flora & Fauna
Dimple 15 Year Old
Bunnahabhain 18 Year Old

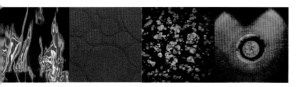

Chocolate and whisky crème brûlée with pan-fried Morello cherries

This sweet stays on the bittersweet side with a high content cocoa chocolate and little sugar in the preparation. The Morello cherries will bring a complement to the dish.

For the crème brûlée
6 egg yolks
50g caster sugar
400ml double cream
50ml semi-skimmed milk
150g dark bitter chocolate
(60% cocoa minimum)
6 tbsp single malt
4 tbsp demerara sugar & 1 tbsp instant
coffee granules (mixed)
For the pan-fried Morello cherries
300g Morello cherries (drained if tinned)
30g salted butter
1 tbsp demerara sugar

Melt the chopped chocolate in a bowl placed over a pan of simmering water (bain-marie). Whisk the caster sugar and egg yolks together. Add the melted chocolate, then the double cream and milk while stirring continuously. Then add the whisky.

Divide equally into individual heatproof dishes (maximum depth 2 cm). Bake in the oven (140°C - Gas mark 1) for 20 to 25 minutes. Heat must be moderate enough to prevent the mixture from rising. They are cooked when they are set with a slight wobble in the middle. Cool and store in the fridge for at least 2 hours.

When the crème brûlée is chilled and completely set, sprinkle with the demerara sugar and coffee mixture. Caramelize with a blow torch or under a hot grill. Return to the fridge.
Before serving, melt the butter in a pan, add the cherries, sprinkle with the demerara sugar and pan-fry for a few minutes on a high heat. Serve them separately in a bowl. If any juice left, reduce it and pour over the cherries.

COOKING TIP
You can add the whisky to the cherries instead of the crème brûlée (in this case, flavour the crème brûlée with vanilla seeds). See how different the dessert tastes, using the same ingredients in a different way. And go for your favourite.

WHISKIES TO MATCH

PROFILE
A whisky (malt or blend) which has been finished in a Port cask will find the perfect harmony with chocolate and cherries. Some fruity sherried malts can also get well with this not too sweet dessert.

SUGGESTIONS
BenRiach 15 Year Old - Tawny Port Wood Finish
Cragganmore Distillers Edition
The Balvenie Port Wood 21 Year Old
The Naked Grouse
Black Bull 21 Year Old

Poached apples with whisky fudge sauce

A typical Autumn sweet, comforting and easy which can be prepared quickly. The spices balance the sweetness of the fudge sauce.

6 sharp tasting apples (e.g Cox Orange)
3 tbsp heather honey
3 tbsp demerara sugar
1 cinnamon stick
3 cloves
2 vanilla pods (cut and opened)
ground black pepper
For the fudge sauce
100g caster sugar
3 tbsp water
1 tsp lemon juice
100 ml double cream
1 egg yolk
30g butter
1 tsp chopped crystallised ginger
2 gingerbread slices
50 ml single malt

Peel, core and cut the apples in half. Place them with the peel in a pan. Cover with water. Add the honey, the demerara sugar and the spices (including vanilla). Bring to the boil and poach the apples until cooked but still holding their shape. Put them aside to cool.

Make the whisky fudge sauce. Make a caramel by heating the sugar, 3 tablespoons water and the lemon juice together. When the syrup gets to golden brown, take it off the heat and slowly add the cream. Put back on the heat to melt any hardened caramel.

Take off the heat and add the egg yolk. Stir well and heat again without bringing to the boil. When the sauce has thickened, take off the heat. Add the butter. Blend gingerbread into fine crumbs. Add to the sauce with the crystallised ginger and the whisky. Stir and leave to cool.

Drain the apples and slice each half apple into the shape of a fan. Decorate with spices (cinnamon stick, cloves and a piece of vanilla pod). Warm the sauce and spoon around the apples. Serve with a shortbread.

COOKING TIP

You can also serve the apples warm, as a gratin. Pour the fudge sauce into a baking dish then place the sliced apples on top. Sprinkle with sugar and place under a grill (not too close) for 8 minutes.

WHISKIES TO MATCH

PROFILE

The best choice will be a spicy and malty whisky. Speyside whiskies would be my favorite as they often offer this cider apple/ tarte Tatin character when matured for more than ten years.

SUGGESTIONS

GlenDronach 12 Year Old Original
Glen Moray 16 Year Old
The Macallan Gold
Aberfeldy 12 Year Old
Strathisla 12 Year Old

Bitter chocolate cake with an orange and whisky sauce

This cake is served warm. It will be crispy outside and melting inside. Adjust the cooking time to your own oven. One minute too much and you will lose the crispy/melting effect.

100g dark chocolate
(minimum 60% cocoa content)
100g unsalted butter
4 eggs
100g caster sugar
60g plain flour (sieved)
For the orange sauce
the grated zest of 2 oranges
the juice of 3 oranges
2 tbsp of thick cut orange marmalade
2 tbsp of caster sugar
1/4 tsp of ground ginger
3 tbsp whisky
For decoration
3 sections of crystallized orange (cut in two)
icing sugar

Melt the chocolate in a bowl placed on top of a saucepan filled with hot water (bain-marie). Add the butter cut into small pieces, stir over a low heat until smooth.
In a separate bowl, whisk the eggs and sugar until the mixture becomes light in colour and thickens. Stir in the flour and the melted chocolate. Butter six ramekins and sprinkle them with caster sugar. Fill with the mixture to 3/4 full. Allow to chill in the fridge for a few hours.

Put the orange zest in a saucepan with the orange juice, the sugar, the marmalade, the ground ginger and 50ml of water. Bring to the boil and reduce on a fast heat for 10 to 15 minutes until a thick sauce is produced. Take off the heat, add the whisky. Allow to chill in the fridge.

Preheat the oven (200 °C - Gas mark 6) about 25 minutes before you are ready to serve the sweet. Place the ramekins on a baking tray and cook for 8 to 10 minutes until the tops have formed a crust and they are starting to come away from the sides of their moulds. Turn out each cake from its ramekin onto a plate (a tricky stage as the heart of the cake is still soft). Pour the orange sauce around the edge of the plate. Add a strip of crystallised orange and sprinkle the icing sugar over the cake.

WHISKIES TO MATCH

PROFILE
Sherried whiskies are a natural option but it is interesting to go on the spicy side, even with a touch of smoke. The oakiness and spices will echo the chocolate and orange bitterness.

SUGGESTIONS
Dailuaine 16 Year Old - Flora & Fauna
Dalmore 12 Year Old
The Spice Tree (Compass Box)
Bowmore Darkest
Talisker Port Ruighe

Chocolate and whisky tart

This dessert is for lovers of pure dark chocolate. It is intense and not sweet. The addition of cardamom brings another dimension to a classic 'ganache'.

For the pastry
40g icing sugar
120g unsalted butter at room temperature
2 tbsp ground almonds
1 pinch of salt
1 egg yolk
200g plain flour
For the ganache
250g dark chocolate
(60% cocoa minimum) roughly chopped
150 ml double cream
the seeds of 10 cardamom pods
2 egg yolks
1 tsp instant coffee granules
40 g unsalted butter
3 tbsp single malt

Preheat the oven (180°C - Gas mark 4).
In a bowl, mix together the icing sugar, the butter, the ground almonds, salt and the egg yolk. Then add the flour and knead together into a pastry dough. Wrap the pastry in cling film and put in the fridge for one hour. Roll out the pastry and line a loose bottomed greased tart tin. Line it with greaseproof paper. Fill it with dry beans to prevent the pastry from swelling. Cook for 20 minutes. Remove paper and beans and cook 10 minutes more. Leave to cool.

Gently toast the cardamom seeds in a dry frying pan for 2 minutes then crush them in a mortar. Slimmer the cream in a saucepan with the crushed cardamom for 5 minutes. Put the chocolate in a large bowl. Sieve the cream and pour it over the chocolate and stir until the chocolate is melted. Add the instant coffee granules and butter.

Keep stirring then add the egg yolks. Leave to cool for 20 minutes. Then add the whisky, stir and place in the fridge for 15 minutes. Take the ganache out of the fridge 15 min before filling the pastry case. Put the tart back into the fridge. Allow the tart to come to temperature room 20 minutes before serving.

WHISKIES TO MATCH

PROFILE
Dark chocolate pair very well with sherried whiskies. The cardamom, with its balsamic/minty flavours, welcomes smoky whiskies and will be enhanced by a spicy malt.

SUGGESTIONS
Aberlour a'bunadh
The Glenlivet 21 Year Old - Archive
Highland Park 18 Year Old
Lagavulin Distillers' Edition
Talisker 18 Year Old

Citrus fruit terrine with a malt/tea jelly

This is an amazing dessert, completely transformed by the addition of a peated malt. Maybe the best demonstration of how deeply whisky can change the taste of a dish!

4 tangerines
2 grapefruit
2 limes
1 lemon
50g caster sugar
one pinch ground black pepper
For the jelly
2 tsp of Earl Grey tea leaves
4 tbsp single or blended malt
5 gelatine leaves
6 mint leaves
For decoration
2 tbsp thin cut orange marmalade
the juice of half an orange
1 tbsp single or blended malt

Soak the gelatine leaves for 10 minutes in cold water to soften them. Infuse the tea leaves for 3 minutes in 200 ml of boiling water. Strain into a bowl then add caster sugar and the drained and squeezed gelatine leaves. Stir until the gelatine leaves are completely melted. Add the citrus fruit juice and the single or blended malt. Stir to marry all the elements together.

Pour the liquid into a loaf tin (approximately 25 x 11 cm) to a depth of 1 cm. Leave to set 10 minutes in the fridge. Place the mint leaves on the surface of the set jelly. Add the fruit segments. Pour the rest of the jelly liquid over the fruit. Leave to set 24 hours in the fridge.

Take one tablespoon of grated zest from each citrus fruit. Peel them above a bowl, collect the juice. Segment the fruit. Place the segments in a separate bowl. Add the grated zest to the juice.

Turn out the terrine, cut into slices and serve on individual plates. For decoration, liquidize the marmalade, the orange juice and the whisky. Spoon around the terrine slice.

WHISKIES TO MATCH

PROFILE
It has to be a heavily peated single or blended malt. The matching of smoke/tar/iodine and citrus fruit is extraordinary.

SUGGESTIONS
Laphroaig 10 Year Old
Ardbeg 10 Year Old
Big Peat - Douglas Laing
Kilchoman Machir Bay
Talisker Storm

Pineapple carpaccio and ginger icecream with a whisky infused syrup

A perfectly ripe pineapple, with the kick of ginger icecream, will bring sunshine to your table on a bleak winter's day. Light, elegant and colourful.

For the carpaccio
A perfectly ripe pineapple (700g)
1 lime (juice and grated zest)
60g caster sugar
1 pinch ground black pepper
(or Sechouan pepper)
2 star anise
3 tbsp single malt
For the icecream
4 egg yolks
100g caster sugar
150ml semi-skimmed milk
300ml double cream
60g crystallised ginger (chopped)
1tbsp ground ginger
sprigs of mint (optional)

Prepare the icecream. If possible, make the custard the day before so that the ginger infuses longer and releases more flavours.
Chop the crystallised ginger very finely. Whisk the egg yolks with sugar until the mixture forms a ribbon. Warm the milk and cream with the ground ginger. Pour the hot milk mixture over the egg yolk mixture, whisking constantly. Return this mixture to a saucepan over low heat. Cook, stirring constantly until the custard thickens and coats the back of a wooden spoon (do not allow custard to boil, as it might curdle). Add the crystallised ginger. Stir and then let cool. Pour the custard in the icecream maker or in a suitable container in the freezer (if using this method, remove from the freezer after one hour and whisk to break up any ice crystals).

Peel the pineapple and cut it as thinly as possible (if you freeze it, it will be easier to cut). You need at least 18 slices.
Make a light syrup, by boiling 100ml of water with the zest and juice of the lime, the caster sugar, the black pepper and star anise. Simmer for 5 minutes, then strain. Leave to cool and add the whisky.

Put three slices of pinapple carpaccio on a dessert plate. Coat with 1 tablespoon of the syrup and put in the fridge. Add a scoop of ginger icecream just before serving.

WHISKIES TO MATCH

PROFILE
The juicy pineapple will find a perfect harmony with a single malt matured in bourbon casks. A finish in a rum cask is an indisputable plus.

SUGGESTIONS
The Balvenie 14 Year Old - Caribbean Cask
BenRiach 15 Year Old - Dark Rum Wood Finish
Glenfiddich 21 Year Old - Gran Reserva
Jack Teeling Small Batch
The Glenlivet Nadùrra 16 Year Old

AMUSE-BOUCHES & MIGNARDISES

Let's have a party

Whisky and nibbles can make a pleasant alternative to a solid meal when you have decided to host a party and invite as many friends as your house can hold. It may not be as easy and straightforward to pair a large selection of finger food with the right whisky. But it is not impossible.

Rather than strict recipes, this chapter offers ideas, suggestions for better enjoying whisky with amuse-bouches (French for a savoury nibble) and mignardises (French for a sweet nibble). I have gathered ideas I developed in different pairing food and whisky events all around the globe. The season theme is still present and the recipes or suggestions bear a logo to identify the season.

Egg sandwich ↗

Cut sandwich bread slices into triangles. Mix grated lemon zest with butter. Butter the bread triangles. Blend three boiled eggs with olive oil, white wine vinegar and herbs (coriander or tarragon). Season with salt and pepper. Place a little piece of salad on each small triangle of bread. Top with the egg mixture.

Smoked salmon rounds ↗

Cut slices of lightly smoked salmon exactly to the size of Walkers mini-oatcakes. Do the same with spinach leaves. Mix mascarpone with juice, add 1 tablespoon of whisky and ground pepper. Spread the mixture on the bread. Top with a spinach leaf and a salmon round. Decorate with a little piece of lemon pulp and a sprig of dill (or chervil).

Lemon curd tartlet ↗

Make lemon curd (see recipe p. 106 but without using gelatin leaves).
Just spread the lemon curd on Walkers mini-shortbread. Add grated lemon zest on the top.

WHISKIES TO MATCH

Go for a young single malt, matured in bourbon casks with a citrussy, grassy and minty or aniseed profile.
Glenrothes Alba Reserve, BenRiach Heart of Speyside, Auchentoshan Classic, Glenfiddich 12 Year Old, Bruichladdich Classic

Carrot salad ☀

See recipe p. 36. Present it in small glasses.

Tomato and chicken brochettes ☀

Marinade chicken cubes in lemon juice with salt and pepper for 15 minutes. Warm a pan with olive oil. Sprinkle almond powder on the chicken cubes and cook them in the pan until golden brown. Thread a cube of chicken, a basil leaf and a cherry tomato on a wooden stick. You can serve a chili sauce to dip the chicken in.

Mini crèmes brûlées ☀

Mix 4 yolks with 50 g caster sugar and 1 teaspoon of vanilla extract until you get a creamy texture, add 400ml of single cream. Pour in small china ovenproof dishes and cook for 10 minutes in the oven (130°C - Gas mark 1/3). When cool, sprinkle with brown sugar and caramelize under the grill.

WHISKIES TO MATCH

Fruit is the key. The summertime dram is fresh but full-bodied. Intensely fragrant and fruity: red fruit or sweet juicy pears, or melon, all notes which have encapsulated sunshine!
The Glenrothes 1991, The Glenlivet Nàdurra Oban 14 Year Old, Cragganmore 12 Year Old The Singleton of Dufftown.

Black pudding toast 🐎

Chop a small sweet onion and caramelize it in honey and butter. Add one green diced apple. Season with salt and pepper. Pan fry 2 slices of black pudding and 'crumble' them. Add the onions and the apple. Divide onto Walkers mini-oatcakes.

Cheese sandwich 🐎

Cut slices of brown bread into four squares. Spread fruit chutney on each (see p. 141). Cover with a thin slice of old cheddar. Alternatively, you can make 'croque-monsieur' with the same ingredients, by topping the cheese sandwich with another square of bread and toasting the sandwich.

Gingerbread snap 🐎

Dry thin slices of gingerbread in the toaster. Cut each slice into four squares. Spread with a homemade apple and pear purée. Sprinkle with cinnamon and toasted hazelnuts.

For a savory alternative: place a thin slice of foie gras on the toasted gingerbread. And cover with a slice of fig which has marinated in red port for a few hours.

WHISKIES TO MATCH

To match the concentrated flavours of the long cooked dishes and candied fruit, we are looking for whiskies with a deep and rich aromatic profile. They will be complex, aged at least 15 Years and they will release sherry notes.
The Macallan Sienna., Mortlach 15 Year Old Highland Park 18 Year Old, Benromach 15 Year Old, Dalmore Cigar Malt

Fruit in disguise ❄

Halve and pit dates. Halve dried apricots. Mix marzipan with lemon juice and whisky. Roll bits of shape of an olive. Stuff the fruits and place them in small paper cups.

Cardamom and chocolate cream with a cappuccino touch ❄

In a bowl, break 110g of dark chocolate into small pieces. Toast the seeds from 6 carda-mom pods in a pan and crush them. Warm 150ml of milk and 50ml of double cream with the cardamom and let infuse 10 minutes then sieve. Whisk 2 egg yolks with 1 tablespoon caster sugar, add warm milk and cream. Put on the stove, making sure it does not boil. When it thickens, take off the stove and pour onto the chocolate. Mix until the chocolate has totally melted. Melt 1tsp instant coffee granules in a few drops of hot water. Whip the cream with icing sugar. Add coffee to this Chantilly cream. Pour the chocolate cream into small glasses. Let cool in the fridge for one hour. Top with the coffee Chantilly cream.

Flapjack ❄

Flapjacks are chewy biscuits made from rolled oats, golden syrup or honey, butter and sugar. You can easily find the recipe on the internet. Or buy them at your baker's.

WHISKIES TO MATCH

The single malts to pair with those wintery delights are quite similar to the ones chosen for Autumn but a bit older. with more oak, longer licoriced finishes and an added sweetness expressed by soft spices and candied fruit. Glenfarclas 30 Year Old, Glenrothes 1978 Linkwood 25 Year Old, Bowmore 25 Year Old Bunnahabhain 25 Year Old

OTHER IDEAS

Duck, gingerbread and orange 🌶

Cut thin gingerbread slices into triangles. Dry them in the oven (110°C - Gas mark 1/4). Mash cooked parsnips) with butter, add orange zest. Season. Top each gingerbread triangle with a teaspoon of vegetable puree, a rasher of un-smoked duck breast (or parma prosciutto) and an orange segment.

WHISKIES TO MATCH

A lightly peated single malt will be perfect. Bowmore 12 Year Old, anCnoc Cutter, Benromach Peat Smoke, Talisker 10 Year Old, Highland Park 12 Year Old.

Whisky chocolate Truffles ❄

For 40 truffles

200g good quality dark chocolate (minimum 60% cocoa content) | 40g salted butter | 1 tsp instant coffee granules | 30g icing sugar
1 egg yolk | 4 tbsp crème fraîche | 60ml single malt | 5 tbsp cocoa powder

Break the chocolate into small pieces into a bowl and melt it over a pan of simmering water (bain-marie). Add butter, instant coffee granules, the egg yolk and icing sugar. Whisk until you get a smooth texture.

Take off the heat, add the crème fraîche little by little. Add the whisky, stir and set aside to in the fridge for a minimum of 3 hours.

When the truffle mix is hard take a teaspoon of mixture, roll it under your fingers in a small ball. Put back in the fridge for one hour.

To finish, roll each ball into cocoa powder. Put each truffle in a paper case. You can keep your truffles eight to ten days in an airtight tin in the fridge.

WHISKIES TO MATCH

Sherried whiskies offer the perfect combination. Even better if they have a peated profile. Lagavulin Distiller's Edition, Talisker 18 Year Old, Bowmore 18 Year Old, Glenrothes Sherry Reserve, Tamdhu 10 Year Old.

After dinner delights

Why not accompany the 'wee deoch an doris' (a last farewell drink) with a shortbread? I was asked by Walkers Shortbread company to find the perfect pairing for their shortbread range with Speyside single malts for the last edition of the Spirit of Speyside Whisky festival.

Although the basic recipe is the same for each biscuit, apart from the Stem Ginger ones, there is a noticeable difference in the flavours, resulting from the different shape and texture of the biscuits. This explains why the whiskies offer different styles.

HOMEBAKE ROUNDS

TASTING NOTES | Very rich in butter. Luscious. Tastes like real homebake. Crumbly, soft, smooth.

PAIR WITH...
'Aberlour 12 Year Old'

Choose an older whisky, dry and crisp. Even a bit oaky. The shortbread will tame the oakiness down.
Go for an all classic "heavier" Speyside mix of sherry and bourbon maturation.

SHORTBREAD FINGERS

TASTING NOTES | The classic. Buttery. Tastes of butter that has been baked. Dense texture with a crisp bite.

PAIR WITH...
'The Glenlivet 12'

Go for a bourbon cask matured whisky. A fruity and sweet whisky with summer-like fragrances.
The smooth and welcoming one: Creamy and smooth with marzipan and fresh hazelnuts.

STEM GINGER SHORTBREAD

TASTING NOTES | Bold and crunchy. Ginger dough with additional tangy candied ginger. The taste of butter comes in the end. The spicy ginger lingers.

PAIR WITH...
'Benromach'

Choose a spicy whisky with sweet sherry influences. Smooth and full bodied with subtle earthy notes. The biscuit pairing will give the whisky a longer finish.

HOMEBAKE FINGERS

TASTING NOTES | Thick and chunky cut. Rich, crumbly. Wheat flour present. Slightly salty, not overly sweet.

PAIR WITH...
'Knockando 12 Year Old'

Choose a dry whisky. The butter will add roundness to the pairing. The dry whisky will lighten the richness of the shortbread.
Go for a malty style. Light, pleasantly sweet. Clean and easy to drink.

STOCKS, SAUCES AND DRINKS

Quick tips and basic sauces

This 'liquid chapter' has no other ambition than giving ideas and tips for better enhancing the dishes with an additional dash of whisky. Rather than detailed recipes, the following pages offer a quick survey of basic sauces and stocks, revisited for the occasion to incorporate whisky or achieve a better matching.

STOCKS

I am not going to give recipes to make stocks. They can easily be found on internet or in cookery books. I just want to make a point here: don't use stock cubes or readymade stocks nor court-bouillons. They just spoil the broth.

There is nothing easier than preparing a good base for a sauce with what is discarded from a meat (bones, fat, skin) or seafood (fishbones, shellfish shells).

A few vegetables, spices, water, sometimes a glass of wine and you let simmer for a good hour.

The best is to make a good quantity of stock ready to freeze in small containers.

Believe me, it is worth the effort.

TOPPINGS

FLAVOURED BUTTER

Soups are usually served with bread and butter. So are specific starters. Why not add the right je ne sais quoi to the dish with an aromatised butter? The butter should not be hard but sit at room temperature for at least one hour before use. Of course choose a very good quality butter. Should I dare say French butter? I personally prefer unsalted butter and I like to add a small pinch of fleur de sel.

Here are some suggestions to accompany dishes.

Herb butter

This will complement a spring dish like the minty green pea velouté p. 28.

Gather a good handful of fresh herbs such as basil, tarragon, flat parsley or chives. Cut them very finely and incorporate into the butter with the fork. You may use your hands to make sure the herbs are evenly incorporated.

With a grassy/malty whisky.

Citrus butter

Very simple, you add grated orange, lime or lemon to the butter, always working in the same way. Excellent on a toasted brioche or on pancakes for breakfast.

With a sherried whisky for the orange or a young bourbon matured one for the lime or lemon.

Seaweed butter

Take dry Japanese seaweeds. Rehydrate them with a peated whisky and incorporate them into the butter with a pinch of fleur de sel.

Ideal to accompany a seafood platter or a plate of oysters.

Spicy butter

Depending on the use you want to do, select a single spice or a mix. Cumin will be perfect to add a knob of butter on a lamb chop, chili and pepper will suit a steak, aniseed will enhance a grilled fish. As for the whisky, it depends on the dish.

CHUTNEYS

Delicious with cheeses, chutneys offer a wide range of possibilities.

Plum and pear chutney

Stone and chop 450g dark red plums. Peel, seed and dice 3 Conference pears.

Chop 100g of sweet onions. Sweat them in butter. Add the fruit and cook for 5 minutes over high heat. Add 100g brown sugar, 150ml cider vinegar and spices (ground ginger, ground cinnamon, ground cloves, ground pepper). Stir and simmer for 45 minutes over low heat until the liquid has nearly totally evaporated and the mixture has thickened. Off the heat, add 5 tablespoons of whisky, stir and pour immediately in airtight jars.

A malty Speysider such as Strathisla 12 year-old will be the perfect option.

To serve with: manchego cheese, lamb kebab, indian rice.

Celery and apple chutney

The method is similar. Use chopped onion, chopped celery sticks, Bramley apples, malt vinegar and apples juice, brown sugar of course and a mix of spices (cinnamon, coriander, allspice). Proceed exactly like for the plum and pear chutney.

A Highland nutty single malt such as Glen Garioch Founder Reserve or a rustic one such as Old Pulteney 12 Year Old will match well with the apple notes and the spices of this chutney.

To serve with a blue cheese or a brocoli and Stilton quiche.

RAISINS IN WHISKY

Practicality inspired me for this very handy recipe. For more than ten years, I tasted the new releases for Whisky Magazine in every issue. I was sent twenty-five samples (blind) every time. I tasted and described each sample. But what to do with all these samples afterwards? It seemed a shame to pour them down in the sink as I could not possible drink them all.

So I started filling jars with sultanas or dried apricots that I would cover with my samples of whisky. That vatted malt - now called blended malt - would include various components: a touch of peat, a touch of sherry, a good malty core etc…

Then I would 'forget' my jars. And try the preserve after a few months. The drenched with whisky raisins were swollen and absolutely delicious.

I use them in salads, in poultry stuffings or in puddings such as cakes or rice pudding. They are a valuable enhancer in daily cooking.

DRESSINGS

In Spring and Summer, we like to invite salads to the table. Raw crunchy vegetables enhanced by the proper dressing become a real delight. At first sight, this type of dish does not seem very appropriate to be matched with whisky. And yet, there are wonderful combinations to create, provided you look a little further than just oil and vinegar.

The strong flavours of mustard, vinegar, horseradish or wasabi require a pungent and dry whisky. The best results are obtained with peated or sherried single malts.

With peated whisky

Go for olive oil, malt vinegar, lemon or lime, mustard, wasabi, herbs, chili, olives.

With sherried whisky

Prefer hazelnut or walnut oil, balsamic vinegar, orange, honey, dried fruit, soft spices.

If the addition of vinegar or citrus fruit brings in too much tartness, a touch of honey or maple syrup will soften the dressing.

Just add one tablespoon of whisky to your dressing, it is enough to transform it.

FRUIT COULIS

Like for stocks, it is much better to prepare your own fruit coulis. Buy seasonal fruits at their best, ripe and juicy, prepare your coulis and freeze in small containers. Make them as natural as possible. Avoid adding sugar, prefer a touch of honey if the fruits are tangy, always add a pinch of ground pepper to enhance the flavours. A fruit coulis is merely a fruit purée that is strained to get rid of skins and pips.

I don't like freezing strawberries, I think they lose their taste. But raspberries and black currants stand the freezer very well, pears, apples and mangos too.

Add the whisky after having slightly warmed the coulis.

Speyside single malts feature very well with orchard fruit, Irish whiskeys with exotic fruit and black currant and light sweet single malts with red fruit.

CUSTARD

I am afraid I will repeat myself. Readymade custard is banned from my kitchen too.

You will find recipes for custard in the dessert chapter.

Don't be afraid to aromatize a basic vanilla custard:

- chocolate (just add melted dark chocolate). whisky to match: Highland Park 15 Year Old.
- coffee (with a strong 'ristretto' espresso). whisky to match: Dalmore 12 year Old.
- praline (with caramelized hazelnuts blended into a fine powder). whisky to match: Glenmorangie 18 Year Old.
- gingerbread (add crumbled gingerbread in the warm custard. whisky to match: Bunnahabhain 18 Year Old.

Custard is the indispensable sauce to be served with the typical Grand Mère French dessert, les oeufs à la neige or île flottante (floating island), light and delicious. You can also easily turn custard into an icecream.

DRINKS

Sir Robert Bruce Lockhart relates in 'Scotch', a book published in 1951 that 'although whisky, in the Highlands at any rate, is still regarded as a spirit not to be adulterated or tampered with, I must admit there were and are recipes for its use as a medecine and also for the final glory of a feast, recipes far more ancient than the blended whisky we drink today. Of these best known are toddy and Athole Brose'.

The famous Toddy is often self prescribed by who is struck down by a nasty cold (or simply on a rainy day!). The ingredients are simple: hot water, honey, a slice of lemon and a good dash of whisky, usually a blended whisky. As for the proportions, it is better to let the drinker decide for himself or herself.

This national Scottish drink has inspired me for a 'choco toddy': just melt dark chocolate with single cream, warm it in a pan, whisk to make it frothy and pour it in a large cup. Then add whisky to your liking, preferably a sherried single malt. Sprinkle with ground cinnamon or nutmeg.

Whisky Delight
Warm two different icecreams in a pan such as a vanilla one and a coffee one. Flavour the vanilla one with a bourbon matured single malt and the other one with a whisky liqueur. Pour the darkest one into a tall glass first, then add the second one. Push a straw in the glass and serve immediately.

Gaelic coffee
This is the Scottish version of the Irish coffee. Pour a good black coffee in a warmed glass, sweeten to your taste (I use sugar lightly), add 15 ml of single malt or whisky liqueur. Stir and top with 1 tablespoon of double cream, very gently poured on the back of a spoon so that it floats on top of the coffee.

ATMOSPHERIC MENUS

ROMANTIC DINNER
My funny Valentine

Carpaccio of scallops, crunchy vegetables
and crab salad
Baked salmon and halibut in a spicy crust
with lemon, butter and ginger sauce
Citrus fruit and whisky terrine, malt/tea jelly

Music Franz Liszt Liebestraum performed
by Arthur Rubenstein
Dance Waltz
Colour Pink and grey
Flowers Peonies
Whisky Caol Ila 12 Year Old

A FRIENDS' PARTY
Let's get together

Velouté of roasted butternut squash
and coconut
Gougère
Cheese platter

Music Pink Floyd
Dance Rock & Roll
Colour Purple and beige
Flowers Heather
Whisky Midleton Dair Ghaelach

BY THE SEA ON A WILD DAY
Shelter from the storm

Oysters in a sea-jelly
Shellfish and Tartufo Risotto
Pears and Stilton tart

Music Beethoven Sonata N°8 op 13
Pathétique performed by David Fray
Dance Swing
Colour White and blue
Flowers Iris
Whisky Laphroaig Quarter Cask

UN DIMANCHE À LA CAMPAGNE
Animal Farm

Old Cheddar and mushroom quiche
Breast of duck in a marmalade and
whisky sauce, quinoa with dried fruit
Pears in whisky flavoured quince jelly
with ricotta mousse

Music Antonin Dvorak, Slavonic Dance
op 46/8 performed by Berliner Philharmoniker
orchestra conducted by Simon Rattle
Dance Folkloric dance
Colour Beige and brown
Flowers Dahlias
Whisky Benromach 15 Year Old

The author
'One of the World's Top Five'

Martine Nouet has been a food and drinks journalist on French national newspapers, written extensively on food and drink internationally, written books on single malt whisky, including the popular 'Les routes des Malts' and for 6 years was editor of 'Whisky Magazine France' where she became known as 'La Reine de L'Alambic' (Queen of the Still). She is currently a regular contributor to the UK edition.
Now a globally sought after taster and commentator, Martine is regarded as one of the leaders in her field and has been described as in 'the world's top five'.

Master of the Quaich

In April 2012, at Blair Castle, she was honoured by Scotland's whisky industry and inducted as a Master of the Quaich, recognising her exceptional contribution to the industry. There are only 147 Masters of the Quaich, from over 2000 worldwide members and Martine lightly asserts she has a unique status as, 'the only blonde French woman to have received this prestigious recognition'. Born in Normandy she now lives and works from her 'croft' on Islay, the island home of eight of Scotland's great single malt distilleries.

IWSC (International Wine and Spirits Competition)

While she mainly writes on whisky she is also a specialist on outstanding eaux-de-vie like Cognac, Calvados, Armagnac and Rum and is annually a judge at the International Wine and Spirit Competition. As Martine puts it, 'having nosed Calvados from my childhood at family dinners, I probably kept the memory of that superb eau-de-vie and came to spirits later'.

Unique Whisky Pairings and Sensory Experiments

When it comes to food pairing with whisky, Martine has become a leader in her field. While the more traditional connoisseurs finally digest previously unheard of ideas of whisky in tandem with various kinds of food, Martine has gone further still, conducting experimental sensory whisky events involving, art, dance and music. During an art and whisky event staged at London's Whisky Exchange in October 2012 the incredulous and the sceptical were blown away by the graphic interpretation of single malt whiskies by two young artists producing finished work in 20 minutes based entirely on her tastings and interaction with the 40 or so guests.
Throughout the year, she runs successful food pairings events around the world, including The Spirit of Speyside Whisky Festival, being awarded the title of Spirit of Speyside Whisky Festival Ambassador in 2015. She regularly attends Groningen whisky festival (WFNN), Fredericton Spirit Festival in New-Brunswick (Canada) and Whisky Lives in Australia.
A happy resident on the island of Islay in Scotland, Martine Nouet thrives on her passion and her zest for life, making this quote her guideline in life : 'Live the life you love and love the life you live'.

With the collaboration of Martin Mitchell, journalist (Food, Drink, Travel)

Martine Nouet relates her travels and experiments on her website : www.martinenouet.com
You can register on the site to receive her newsletter

The photographer John Paul

John Paul has been a professional photographer since 1982. His work has been published widely throughout the world. Trained as commercial photographer in Glasgow, he chose to work for national newspapers and magazines covering major news throughout the 1980s and 1990s. His career took a turn when he discovered the world of whisky. He is now concentrating on projects in the Whisky food and fashion industries. John Paul works intensely in Speyside as he now lives in Inverness with his Dutch partner.

John Paul has earned an indisputable reputation for the quality and the artistic inspiration of his photos but he is also well-known for his kindness and enthusiasm which are appreciated by all his customers in the whisky industry and beyond. Working with him is a real delight. I met John ten years ago when we prepared the Aberlour whisky dinner during the Spirit of of Speyside Festival. I have admired his artistic flair and great professional competence since then. I am carried away by his shooting for my book ".

www.johnpaul.photography

The Chef Eric Obry

Eric Obry is a talented French chef. After working in several Michelin star restaurants in France, Eric's passion for whisky brought him to Scotland where he fell in love with Speyside. Eric set up the restaurant La Faisanderie in Dufftown and successfully ran the restaurant for fiteen years, gaining a reputation for being one of the finest restaurants in Moray.

With the addition of a young family and the desire for a more family friendly work life balance, Eric and his partner Morag launched a Pâtisserie and Coffee shop in Aberlour. Le Petit Gourmand opened its doors in July 2015 and was an instant hit thanks to the delicious meals and pâtisseries on offer, giving customers an authentic taste of France. The popularity of the pâtisserie heralded the addition of a skilled French pâtissier, who joined the team at Le Petit Gourmand in October 2015. Prior to working at Le Petit Gourmand, the pâtissier worked in Paris, he too was also drawn to Scotland's for its many charms.

Le Petit Gourmand continues to go from strength to strength... review headlines include 'A Jewel in the Crown of Speyside', 'Amazing Patisserie', 'Pastry Chef Extraordinaire!' and 'C'est splendide!'.

I met Eric twelve years ago when we designed the Aberlour Whisky Dinners, one of the highlights of the Spirit of Speyside Whisky Festival. We shared a passion for fine food and found the perfect match with John Paul the photographer. Hence this book which epitomizes our professional affinities and a solid friendship too.

Le Petit Gourmand
The Square
Aberlour AB38 9PX
Morayshire - Scotland

WALKERS SHORTBREAD,
120 YEARS DEDICATED TO QUALITY

Nestled in the scenically stunning Scottish Highlands in Aberlour, Speyside, where Joseph Walker opened his first village bakery in 1898, Walkers remain faithful to its historic roots with Joseph's grandchildren and great-grandchildren continuing the tradition of fine baking, using the original recipe and only the finest ingredients – a policy that has earned the company a global reputation for quality and excellence.

1898-1930 / Walkers Origins

The Walkers story begins in 1898 when the twenty-one year old Joseph Walker opened the doors of his own bakery with a loan of £50 and the ambition to bake 'The World's Finest Shortbread'. In the first year of business, Joseph concentrated on perfecting his shortbread recipe. It was time well spent. Soon, shooting parties from the local estates were making detours just to visit his bakery. As word spread and demand for his quality shortbread increased, Joseph took the first steps to expanding the business by moving to a larger shop in the Speyside village of Aberlour and investing in a horse and cart to deliver his baking further afield.

1930-1950 / The War Years

During the 30s, the business – like Joseph's family – was expanding. Two of his sons – James and Joseph – joined the company, bringing fresh ideas with them.
By 1936 they had introduced three valuable additions to the Walkers setup: a range of cakes, a selection of confectionery and…the company's first delivery van. Now that Walkers produce could be sold at ever-greater distances the prospects for expansion were looking promising.
Then came the war. In spite of wartime rationing and their commitment to the Home Guard, Joseph's sons managed to keep the business going and their customers happy.

1950-1970 / From Aberlour to Harrods

While some manufacturers began to cut corners by using margarine instead of butter, Joseph believed that people still appreciated the care that went into making a superior product like Walkers shortbread. And he was right. That's why his sons remained true to this winningly simple recipe consisting of just four ingredients: flour, sugar, salt and that pure creamery butter. As demand grew so did the business. By 1961, all three of James' children - Joseph, James and Marjorie - had joined the company, making the third generation of Walkers working for the family firm. The workforce was now almost one hundred, and Walkers had a fleet of 14 vans as well as shops in Grantown and Elgin. Soon their shortbread was on the shelves of fine food stores all over Britain. By the 1970s, Joseph's grandchildren had begun exporting Walkers shortbread to over 60 countries around the world – all of it still baked to his original recipe.

1970 until now / Growing Success

By 1975 Walkers had outgrown their extended bakery and moved to a custom built factory. Many of the people who worked for Walkers during this time are still with the company today; most are local folk who often come from the same family - mothers working alongside daughters, fathers and sons. Now, as a hundred years ago, Walkers test every new product in Aberlour's village shop. Though today customers are based all over the world, products are still given their first seal of approval by the villagers of Aberlour. The way to ensure that each cake and biscuit offers a real taste of Scotland.

In addition to pure butter shortbreads, Walkers produce a range of delectable Scottish delicacies, from savoury oatcakes to rich moist fruit cakes and gourmet biscuits. Staying at the forefront of innovation, Walkers continually develops new products such as gluten free shortbread or three seed oatcakes.

For their shortbread as well as for their oatcakes and all their biscuits and cakes, Walkers still use only the finest pure ingredients with no artificial colour, flavourings or preservative.

To discover the whole range
of Walkers Shortbread offer,
visit their website:
www.walkersshortbread.com

The World's Finest Shortbread

INDEX ALPHABETICAL ORDER

INDEX BY SEASON

WHISKY INDEX

CONVERSION TABLES

Oven **temperature conversion table**

Gas	Mark	Fahrenheit Celsius	Description
1/4	225	110	Very cool/very slow
1/2	250	130	-
1	275	140	cool
2	300	150	-
3	325	170	very moderate
4	350	180	moderate
5	375	190	-
6	400	200	moderately hot
7	425	220	hot
8	450	230	-
9	475	240	very hot

Weight conversion table

Weight	Grams to Imperial
10g	1/4oz
15g	1/2oz
30g	1oz
60g	2oz
90g	3oz
125g	4oz (1/4 lb)
155g	5oz
185g	6oz
220g	7oz
250g	8oz (1/2 lb)
280g	9oz
315g	10oz
345g	11oz
375g	12oz (3/4 lb)
410g	13oz
440g	14oz
470g	15oz
500g (1/2 kg)	16oz (1 lb)
750g	24oz (1 1/2 lb)
1kg	32oz (2 lb)
1.5kg	48oz (3 lb)
2kg	64oz (4 lb)

Volume conversion table
Liquids Metric to Cup and Imperial

Metric	Cup	Imperial
30ml		1 fl oz
60ml	1/4 cup	2 fl oz
80ml	1/3 cup	2 3/4 fl oz
100ml		3 1/2 fl oz
125ml	1/2 cup	4 fl oz
150ml		5 fl oz
180ml	3/4 cup	6 fl oz
200ml		7 fl oz
250ml	1 cup	8 3/4 fl oz
310ml	1 1/4 cups	10 1/2 fl oz
375ml	1 1/2 cups	13 fl oz
430ml	1 3/4 cups	15 fl oz
475ml		16 fl oz
500ml	2 cups	17 fl oz
625ml	2 1/2 cups	21 1/2 fl oz
750ml	3 cups	26 fl oz
1L	4 cups	35 fl oz
1.25L	5 cups	44 fl oz
1.5L	6 cups	52 fl oz
2L	8 cups	70 fl oz
2.5L	10 cups	88 fl oz

You can easily find conversion tables on internet and even use online unit converters. Here are websites clear and easy to use:

www.taste.com.au/
www.convert-me.com/
www.goodtoknow.co.uk/

SOME FAVORITES OF MINE

Every keen cook has favorite ingredients they use constantly. I have mine too. I find it interesting to present them and point out why they are worth looking for. It is now much easier to get 'exotic' food through online shops, wherever we are in the world. With a touch of perseverance, one should be able to track these aromatic treasures. It is always possible to find a substitute. But it it is worth the effort to 'try a little harder' as the song says.

Bramley apples

These large bright green apples (not to be confused with Granny Smith) appeared in a Nottinghamshire garden in 1846. The garden was then bought by the local butcher called Matthew Bramley and the seedlings were developed by a local nurseryman. The fruit became very successful. Amazingly, the original Bramley tree still exists and bears fruit every year. Bramleys are the best apples for cooking. They have a higher acid content, hence their tangy flavour is perfect for savoury dishes accompaniments or sauces. Their moist texture is also a plus for pureed preparations. They are ideal for crumbles or tarts.

Espelette Chili

The piment d'Espelette is grown in the southwest of France, in the Basque country, at the frontier with Spain. This variety of chili was brought to France in the 16th century and the small village of Espelette made it its speciality. Now it is also cultivated in the villages around. It was granted a protected status with the AOC (appellation d'origine contrôlée) in 2000. A key ingredient in piperade, a summer vegetable specialty from the Pays basque, Espelette chili can be bought ground and will be used as or instead of pepper. It is not burning nor fiery and it releases a warm smoky flavour.

Fleur de sel

Could I live without my Fleur de sel ? Probably not. This exquisite salt is dangerous. Once you have tasted it, you become addicted. Fleur de sel (flower of salt) comes from the top crust of salt which is harvested in the salt marshes around the city of Guérande, south of Brittany. These tiny sea salt flakes have a delicate flavour and a crunchy feel. Fleur de sel is better used to season a cooked dish rather than added during cooking. Other regions of France and other countries produce fleur de sel now.

French butter

As a Norman 'bred' on farm butter and fresh cream, I have kept the nostalgia of this rich bright yellow butter which had such a distinctive nutty flavour. I cannot use British or Irish butter for pastry. Sorry. Fortunately, the local grocery shop on Islay carries French butter. I can survive!

Olivier Roellinger Spices

My 'mentor' in spices is Olivier Roellinger, one of France best chefs who has now decided to focus on his spice creations. In 'La Maison du voyageur' at Cancale (Brittany), he creates his spice mixes to which he gives poetical names. 'Spices should never be used as single, they should be blended', Olivier Roellinger says, adding: 'Produces are the words of the sentence, and spices its punctuation, they give the dish all its meaning'. His spice mixes are a magnetic sensory world for me. The spices can be bought online.
www.epices-roellinger.com

Stornoway Black pudding

This is the best black pudding in Scotland. Produced on the Isle of Lewis (Outer Hebrides off the west coast), around the town of Stornoway, it has been granted a protected status with a Protected Geographical Indication. It is produced following a traditional recipe: pig's blood is blended with oatmeal, spices and fresh onion. Moist and firm in texture, Stornoway black pudding has little fat, with the perfect level of spiciness. A real treat.